CW00676379

BUILDING
TITANIC
BELFAST

BUILDING TITANIC BELFAST

The Making of a Twenty-First-Century Landmark

PAUL CATTERMOLE

Consulting editors
CLAUDE COSTECALDE
JOHN PAUL DOHERTY

TITANIC BELFAST
PUBLICATIONS

Titanic Belfast Publications would like to dedicate this book to the working men and women of Belfast, past and present, who helped create both *Titanic* and this new home for her memory.

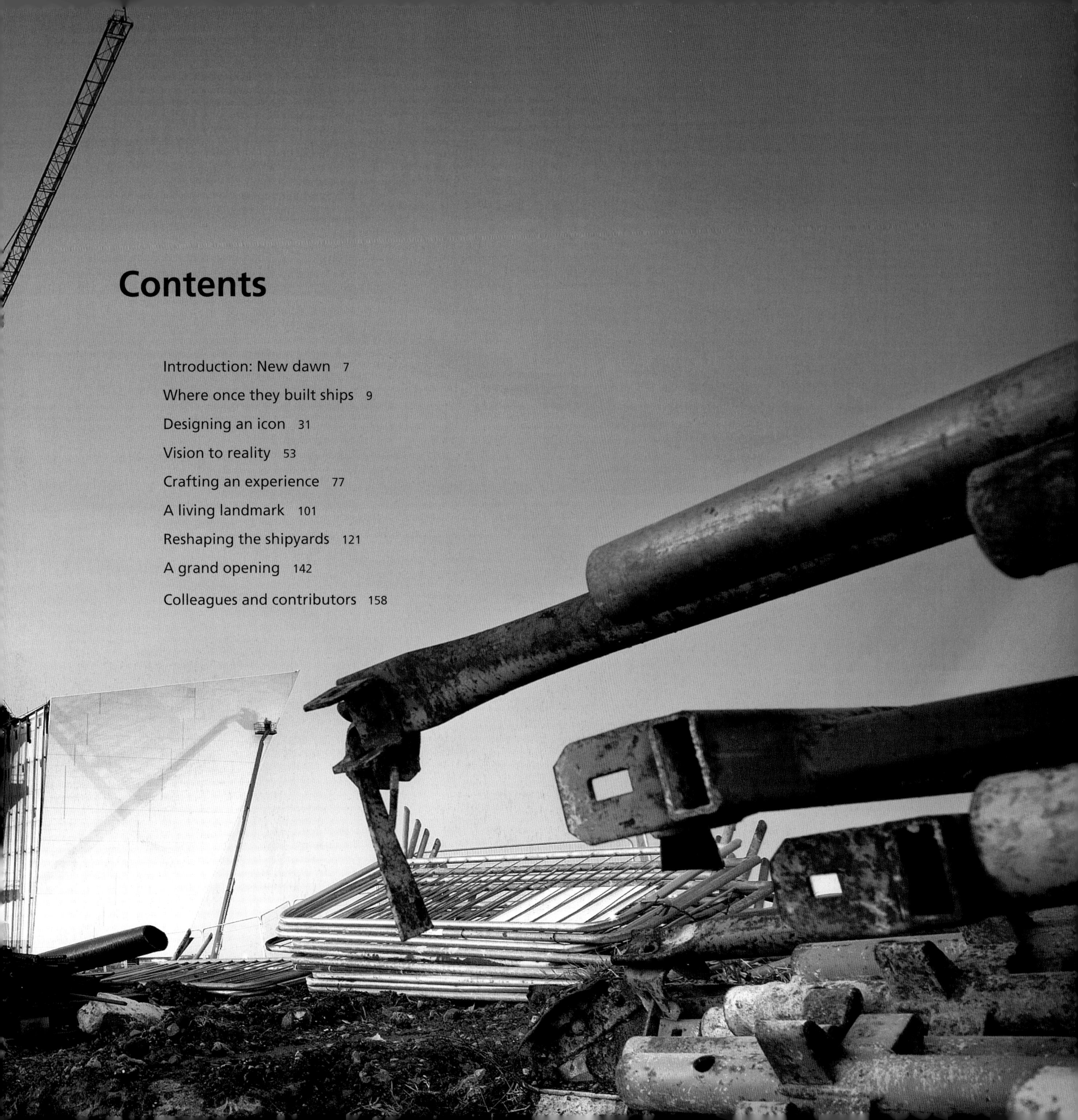

Contents

Introduction

New dawn

Belfast now has two icons – built a century apart, but bound together by history.

The story of *Titanic* and her sinking remains the stuff of legend. It is a story that has been told and retold the world over for the past hundred years, yet it is only in the recent past that her name has been heard mentioned in the very city that gave her form. The largest ship of her day, she embodied the Edwardian world and its spirit of unstoppable progress, but her humbling at the hands of nature made *Titanic* a shameful memory for the community that built her. The ship they had proudly waved out of Belfast Lough became synonymous with the hubris of humanity.

Though the ship proved fallible, the story proved immortal, and the names of those who conceived, commissioned, constructed and commanded her have become integral to the *Titanic* myth. Personalities such as Pirrie, Carlisle, Andrews, Smith and Ismay make up the cast of determined characters who gave the world an engineering wonder. At the dawn of a new millennium, and with the ship's centenary fast approaching, the time was right to re-evaluate that story and set the record straight. It was time for the collective memory of *Titanic* to come home.

A slice of social history, standing in the midst of Belfast's industrial heartland, Titanic Belfast helps restore a city's pride in its achievements, and rightly reclaims its legacy as one of the greatest workshops the world has ever known. In constructing a new signature for Belfast, the attraction's creators have forged many parallels with their Edwardian counterparts, likewise striving to convert vision into reality. The result is a living monument that celebrates the city's past, while also presaging its future.

This book seeks to form a permanent record of this collective effort to build a landmark that would do justice to Belfast's great industrial legacy, and set Queen's Island on course to become a twenty-first century city quarter. This is the story of Titanic Belfast, and the many hands that built her.

Paul Cattermole

APRIL 2013

The end of the newly restored slipways offers a public vantage point from which to watch the sunrise slowly creep down Belfast Lough to the former shipyards of Queen's Island. The central projecting concrete spur shown here once contained the pumping machinery used to drain the extremities of the slips when the temporary cofferdams were in place.

SKYLIFT
Genie S-125

Where once they built ships

This is Titanic Belfast: the world's largest *Titanic*-themed visitor attraction and the centrepiece of Belfast's emerging Titanic Quarter. Memorials and museums devoted to this famous liner can be found across the globe, but it is Belfast that holds the greatest claim to be her spiritual home. Yet, even though *Titanic* was conceived, designed, constructed and launched from this stretch of reclaimed land at Belfast's heart, it was by no means inevitable that such a landmark should come to be built here. Buildings, like the great liners of the Edwardian era, require determined people to will them into being – visionaries to conceive them, designers to draw them and contractors to construct them. This is their story.

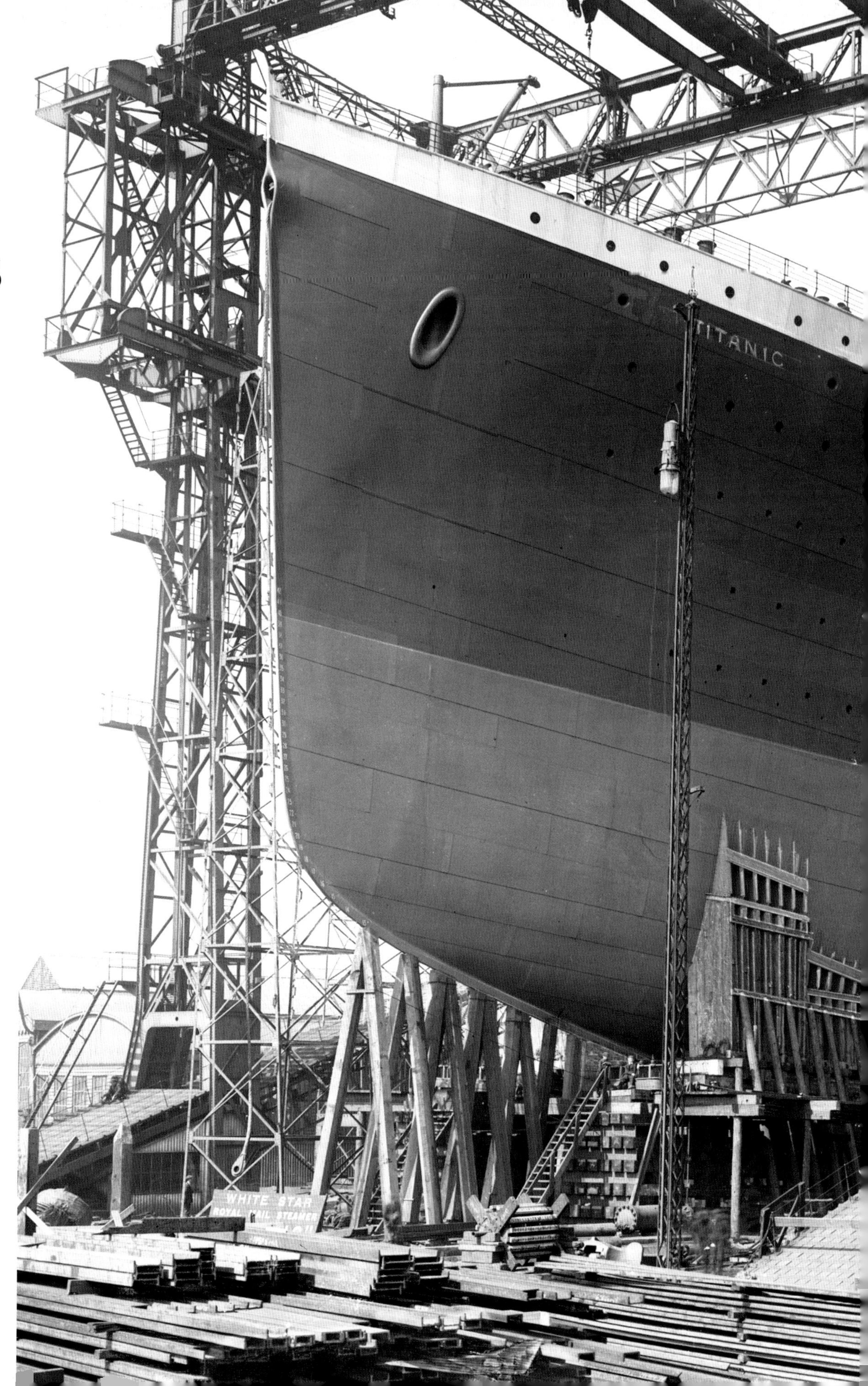

Separated by almost a hundred years, these shots, taken in January 2011 and May 1911, eloquently express the visual parallels between the construction of Titanic Belfast and that of *Titanic* herself. Aluminium panels have superseded steel plates, while tower cranes have replaced gantry pylons, but the tapered hull forms projecting out above Queen's Island remain remarkably similar.

A new beginning

Why visit Belfast? This would have been the likely question on many tourists' lips at the start of the twenty-first century, if a trip to Northern Ireland's capital was suggested to them at all. They would have been well aware of the city's existence, for Belfast's name was in the news often enough – but for all the wrong reasons. Thirty years of the Troubles had made the city synonymous with sectarian strife, the clash of military and militants, and a depth of social unrest that appeared entirely incompatible with casual sightseeing or relaxing weekend breaks. In the collective mindset Belfast was, as the *Lonely Planet* guide says in retrospect, 'lumped with Beirut, Baghdad and Bosnia as one of the four 'Bs' for travellers to avoid'. It was a 'war zone' on the doorstep of the British mainland – where tourists feared to tread.

But change was in the air. After years of seemingly intractable unrest, the mid-1990s saw a concerted effort from across the political spectrum to bring peace to Northern Ireland. A long series of talks, negotiations, ceasefires and conferences culminated in the signing of the Good Friday Agreement in 1998. Also known as the Belfast Agreement, this document set out a framework for a devolved government where all parties could be represented. It was swiftly endorsed by the voting public in a referendum held a little over a month later. It was clear that the collective will to transform Northern Ireland was alive and well. Now that same willpower had to be applied to its shattered tourism industry.

Looking north-east along the line of the Victoria Channel, this aerial photograph records Belfast as it was in 1997 on the eve of the Good Friday Agreement. At its centre lies the Queen's Island works of Harland & Wolff, with the old platers' sheds of the former North and South Yards still lining the river's edge, as they did when *Titanic* was being constructed.

Signature strategy

In late 2003 the Northern Ireland Tourist Board (NITB) issued a significant document under the heading *Tourism in Northern Ireland: A Strategic Framework for Action 2004–2007*. In his foreword, MP Ian Pearson (then Minister for Enterprise, Trade and Investment) summed up the pervading sense that this was the moment to reverse decades of lost trade:

> We live in a new Northern Ireland. There is now a unique and timely opportunity for tourism to take a lead as we go forward ... This will only happen if we develop and market a world-class visitor experience.

But what kind of experience would that be, and how would it be developed? Part of the framework's ten-point plan called for the development of five so-called 'Signature Projects' – themes or attractions 'identified for their potential to deliver world-class excellence, drawing visitors from home and overseas'. These five were: the Giant's Causeway and the wider Antrim and Causeway coast area; the walled city of Derry; Ireland's Christian heritage/St Patrick; the Mournes National Park area; and *Titanic* (maritime)/Belfast.

RMS *Titanic*. The most famous ship in history. The ship that had caught the world's attention when she sank dramatically on her maiden voyage in 1912. The ship that caught the public imagination once more when Dr Robert Ballard discovered her wreck in 1985, and yet again in 1997 when James Cameron's film of the same name became the first to gross over a billion dollars at the box office. The ship whose name forms the basis of countless analogies and has spawned still more myths and legends. The ship that was designed and built in Belfast, by Belfast men, on Belfast soil. Yes, the theme of *Titanic* would be worth investigating.

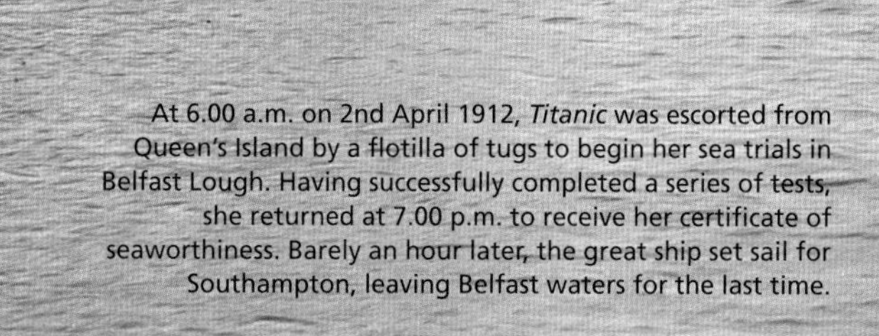

At 6.00 a.m. on 2nd April 1912, *Titanic* was escorted from Queen's Island by a flotilla of tugs to begin her sea trials in Belfast Lough. Having successfully completed a series of tests, she returned at 7.00 p.m. to receive her certificate of seaworthiness. Barely an hour later, the great ship set sail for Southampton, leaving Belfast waters for the last time.

Time and place

The timing of NITB's document was significant, for politics and history had contrived to produce a golden opportunity. If prompt action were taken, there was still time to build an international visitor attraction whose opening could coincide with the centenary of *Titanic*'s fateful maiden voyage. Each of the proposed Signature Projects had promise, but the *Titanic*/maritime concept was the only one founded in industry. It was also specific to Belfast. The plan was effectively looking back, past the recent history that had put paid to any serious tourist trade, to a time when Belfast could rightly claim a place in the pantheon of great world cities.

Prosperous, populous and productive, Edwardian Belfast was a powerhouse of industry and commerce and an engine of the British Empire, though a proportion of its residents would have winced at this metaphor. What was beyond dispute, however, was the legacy of invention and technical achievement in engineering and manufacturing to be found within the city's boundaries. This was something worth celebrating. If this rich seam of narrative could be tapped, then Belfast would come one step closer to reconciling itself to *Titanic*'s tragedy. And, through the enduring appeal of its most famous product, the city would also be able to put itself back on the tourist trail.

A sea of flat caps flows down Queen's Road as Harland & Wolff's 15,000 employees leave the yard on a May evening in 1911. Commanding the skyline behind them is the outline of the Arrol Gantry, with *Titanic*'s hull nearing completion on No. 3 slip.

First steps to greatness

To understand how Edwardian Belfast became a colossus of the shipbuilding world, we must look back over 200 years to a series of far-sighted decisions that helped set the city on the road to fame and fortune. Late-eighteenth-century Belfast was a thriving port, trading linen, corn, cotton and cattle products for coal, tobacco and wine. Yet the harbour itself was by no means ideal, for the shallow River Lagan was barely half a metre deep around the limited stretches of quayside. This placed great restrictions on the kind of vessels that could navigate the channel, requiring ocean-going ships to anchor three miles downriver in the deeper Pool of Garmoyle. Their cargoes would then be laboriously decanted onto smaller barges and lighters to be ferried to the town. These added handling charges greatly increased costs and reduced profits. Belfast's business community was painfully aware that the future prosperity of the port would depend upon its improvement.

The crucial first step in the process was the creation of the Ballast Board by act of parliament in 1785. Its 15 members were tasked with 'Preserving and Improving the Port and Harbour of Belfast'. To fund this endeavour they were permitted to dredge the shallow channel and sell the collected gravel as ballast to merchant ships at two shillings a ton. From these humble beginnings, amongst the mud and silt of the River Lagan, emerged the collective spirit of enterprise that would change the face of Belfast forever.

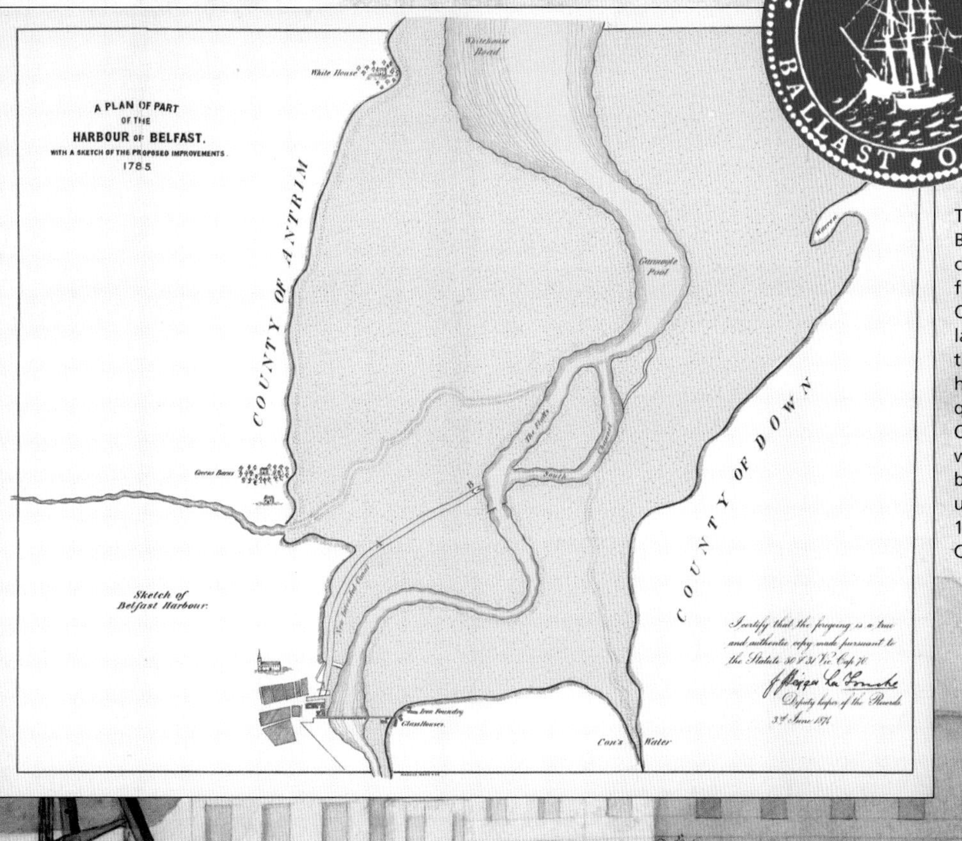

This retrospective sketch map shows the River Lagan as it would have appeared when the Ballast Board was established in 1785. The narrow channel of the Lagan meandered through a sea of silt and mud, presenting a major challenge for navigation. One of many proposed solutions, the ship canal that can be seen bypassing the river's final bends was never built.

The common seal of the Ballast Board was commissioned at their first meeting on 25th October 1785. It depicts a large merchant ship of the kind they hoped to help reach Belfast's quays. The old Ballast Office on Donegall Quay was the venue for the board's regular meetings until it was demolished in 1854 to make way for the Customs House.

Straightening the Lagan

Limited financial resources and rudimentary dredging equipment hampered the Ballast Board's early efforts, for they were reliant on labourers excavating the channel with spades at low tide or scouring the riverbed with a leather bag attached to an iron hoop on a pole. Progress was painfully slow and after ten years the minimum depth of the channel had been increased by only 0.6 metres, and navigation remained difficult. In spite of this hindrance, by 1814 the port's revenue from customs duties approached £400,000 and both the board and the Commissioners of Customs decided to seek a fresh perspective. Over the next 16 years they consulted a series of respected engineers, including Thomas Telford, John Rennie and his son, Sir John Rennie. They all proposed to bypass the shallows with various costly permutations of ship canals and basins, accessed by imposing locks to counteract the tidal waters.

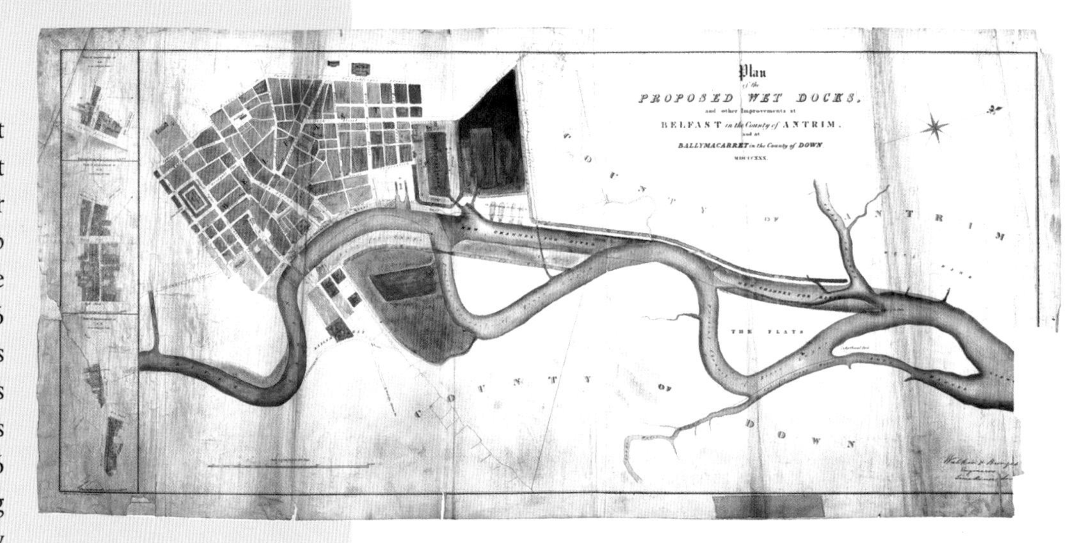

The vivid green washes of Walker's original 1830 plan (above) show how the three bends of the River Lagan would be rationalised into a single channel. Excavated as an arrow-straight line by Dargan's navvies, the Victoria Channel officially opened on 10th July 1849. The name chosen for the new channel anticipated the young queen's official visit to the city the following month.

For all their acumen, these great engineers could not produce a plan that fitted the purse of the Belfast merchants, for the government refused to contribute, and the board's income was far too modest to fund the escalating estimates of up to £400,000. Money was proving to be as great a barrier as mud to Belfast's growth. However, in 1830 a London-based engineer, James Walker of Walker & Burges, finally offered a cost-effective solution. He proposed to dredge a single channel composed of two cuttings through the mud flats, thereby connecting the Pool of Garmoyle directly to the town's quays. Split into affordable phases and estimated to cost between £180,000 and £200,000 (equivalent to over £19 million today), this was a far more realistic proposal. However, it still took another nine years for the necessary authority and funding to be put in place.

Royal assent for the board's grand plan swiftly followed the accession of Queen Victoria in 1837, and the job was put to tender. They selected William Dargan, then Ireland's foremost engineering contractor, who started the first cut ('Dargan's Cut', as it was known locally) in 1839 and completed the task by January 1841. Excavating this first cut generated vast amounts of spoil (commonly referred to as 'slob'), and the board permitted Dargan to deposit this on the south side of the new channel. In the process he gradually fashioned a seven-hectare island that came to bear his name. Dargan successfully completed Walker's second cut between 1846 and 1849 and the harbour's new approach was duly christened the Victoria Channel. The long-term effects of creating both a navigable channel and large areas of reclaimed land were to be dramatic, for this opened the door to greater wealth through expanded trade and industry.

Having completed the Victoria Channel, engineer William Dargan (1799–1867) became the dominant figure in the construction of Ireland's railways throughout the 1850s, at one time employing some 50,000 men. Highly regarded by his peers for both his philanthropy and his business achievements, Dargan's legacy to the arts is commemorated by a statue outside the National Gallery of Ireland, which he helped establish.

Queen's Island's crystal centre

Queen Victoria's 11-day tour of Ireland from 2nd to 12th August 1849 included visits to Cork, Dublin and Belfast. Sailing into Belfast on 11th August, accompanied by Prince Albert and their children, she was warmly received by the whole town – despite the backdrop of ongoing political tensions caused by the Irish Famine and growing nationalist sentiment.

The island that William Dargan created in 1841 was to have as great an impact on Belfast's history as the channel from which its slobland came. At first the Ballast Board was content to set much of Dargan's Island aside for public recreation, planting it with trees to create the People's Park. Throughout the 1840s it played a prominent part in Belfast's public life, climaxing in 1850 with the highly successful Victoria Fete. This was held exactly a year after the monarch's visit, for which occasion the site had been officially renamed Queen's Island. The financial success of the fete funded the construction of one of Belfast's great lost buildings: the Crystal Palace. Designed by John Boyd, this pavilion was built from wood, iron and glass in a similar manner to Joseph Paxton's famous Crystal Palace in London. Measuring 112 feet in length, 72 feet in width and 20 feet in height, the palace opened on 4th September 1851 and became the glittering heart of this oasis of green, set amongst the gritty docks and shipyards. Queen's Island would one day reclaim this verdant past.

This modern watercolour by Diana Oxlade is based upon the only known detailed depiction of the Crystal Palace's exterior, drawn by David Wilkie Raimbach, Assistant Master at the Belfast Government School of Design. Commissioned in May 1851, Raimbach's drawing was derived from John Boyd's architectural plans and shows a dome that, owing to lack of funds, was never realised.

This magnificent *Bird's Eye View of Belfast* by the lithographer J.H. Connop provides a fine impression of Queen's Island as it was in 1863. From 1849 the island assumed a dual identity, with the park to the east and ship-repair facilities to the west. By 1863 these activities had expanded to become a shipyard specialising in the construction of iron vessels, under the ownership of Edward James Harland and Gustav Wilhelm Wolff.

A long pond for storing cut, unseasoned timber formed the southern spine of the island, overlapping both zones of activity. The Crystal Palace sat at the centre of the landscaped pleasure-ground, ringed by tree-lined waterfront promenades. The expanding shipyard may have erased these early gardens, but Queen's Island would eventually rise again as a popular leisure destination.

Shipyards come to rule Queen's Island

The light of the Crystal Palace was to be short lived. Like its famous London counterpart, it was consumed by fire. The blaze of 1864 destroyed the collections of rare plants and birds that had drawn the crowds and, with repairs estimated at half the original construction costs, this icon was left to stand in ruins.

The passing of the palace cleared the way for an important industry to expand eastwards across the island. The Ballast Board had always recognised the island's commercial potential, and their reconstitution as the Belfast Harbour Commissioners in 1847 gave them more powers to pursue this agenda. To give industry a foothold, they had ordered the construction of a patent slip and a timber pond in 1849, expanding the facilities of the port beyond the confines of the old quays. In 1853 the Harbour Commissioners took the momentous decision to spend a further £1,116 17s 6d on fitting out a brand-new shipyard alongside the island's patent slip. This was to be leased to a Robert Hickson, 'with the object of encouraging Iron Shipbuilding on a more extensive scale than previously'. Few could then have imagined how extensive this industry would become.

By 1858 Hickson's yard had built four iron sailing ships, two iron steamships and a paddle tug, but a dip in the economy damaged his finances. He offered to sell his business to his energetic young manager, Edward Harland, who had joined him in 1854. Harland accepted, and the firm was duly renamed Edward James Harland & Company. The £5,000 purchase was funded by his friend, G.C. Schwabe of Liverpool, whose nephew Gustav Wolff was Harland's personal assistant.

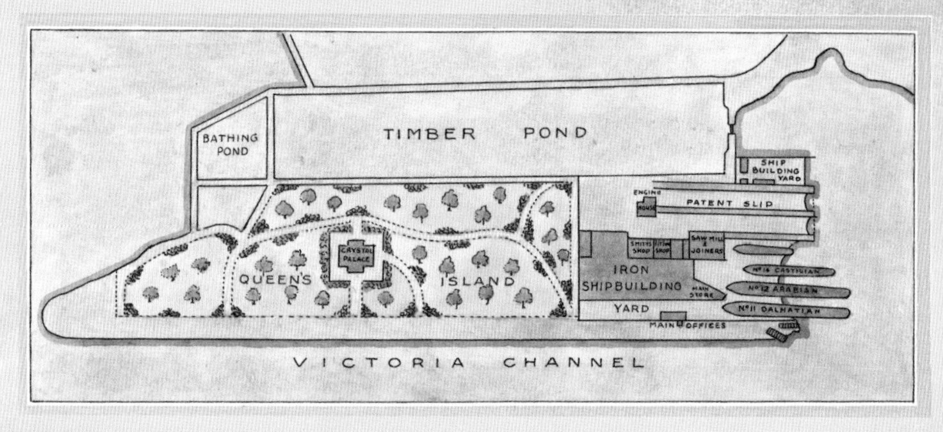

This watercolour map of 1862 depicts a south-facing view of Queen's Island the year after Edward Harland and Gustav Wolff entered into a formal partnership, bringing the legendary firm of Harland & Wolff into being. Beside their yard was the important patent slip or marine railway – an inclined plane with large cradles mounted on rails running into water that could be used to draw ships out of the river for repairs.

Completed for J. Bibby & Company in 1859, the graceful *Venetian* was the first vessel to be designed and constructed by Edward James Harland & Company. Although built of iron and fitted with steam propulsion, she still carried a full sailing rig, for sail continued to supplement steam for decades until the improved reliability and economics of maritime engines made canvas redundant.

Robert Hickson & Company successfully launched the 1,000-ton *Norah Graeme* from their Queen's Island yard on 13th February 1858. Hickson had pioneered iron shipbuilding on the island, but just seven months after this launch he sold his business to Edward Harland, marking the beginning of an even greater enterprise.

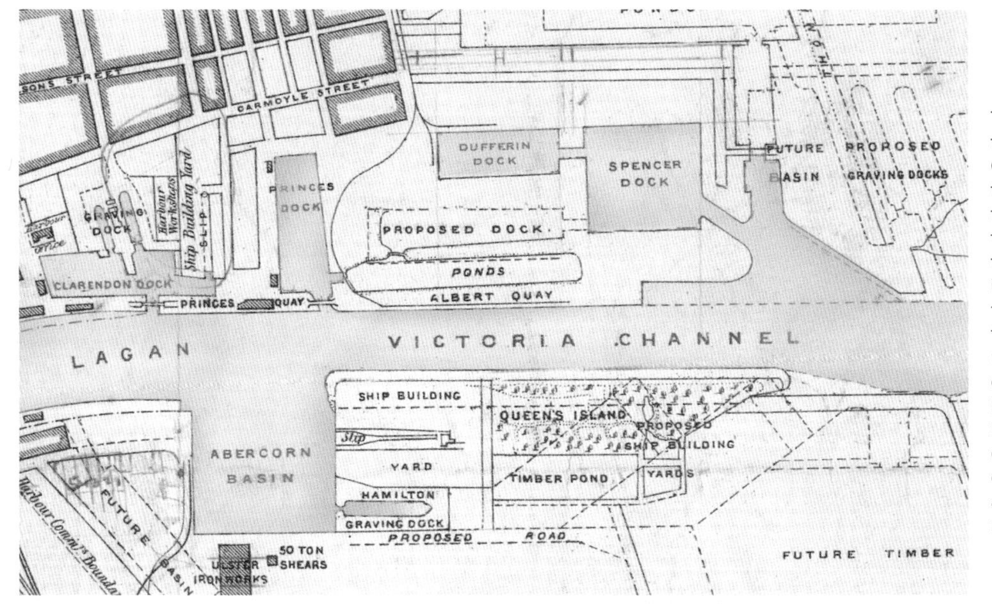

The historic port maps of the Belfast Harbour Commissioners all place the Victoria Channel on the horizontal, rather than orientating it to true north. Mentally inverting the south-facing 1862 map on the opposite page, the wedge-shaped outline of the People's Park can still be traced in this map of 1872, despite the eastern end of the island being absorbed into a mass of newly reclaimed land.

By the time Edward Harland became Chairman of the Belfast Harbour Commissioners in 1875, he employed over a thousand workers and had produced more than 100,000 tons of shipping. His one-hundredth vessel, the paddle steamer *Princess Beatrice*, was launched the same year he took office. Painted in 1884, this brooding portrait supports Harland's reputation as an imposing captain of industry. His achievements did not go unnoticed, for he was both knighted and granted a baronetcy the following year.

As well as financing the fledgling company, Wolff's uncle was to provide some of the firm's most important early commissions, ordering no fewer than 11 ships for his Bibby Line. These were delivered between 1859 and 1862. Harland was an innovative shipbuilder, patenting the use of iron decks and evolving long, narrow hulls with flat bottoms that gave his vessels both greater stability and greater capacity. A talented draughtsman himself, Wolff went into full partnership with Harland in 1861. The pairing proved highly successful. The close ties with the Bibby Line became the template for future business relationships, the most enduring of which was with Thomas Ismay's White Star Line. The first vessel to be built by Harland & Wolff for the White Star Line was the iron sailing barque *Broughton*, completed and delivered in 1867 with help of financial backing from G.C. Schwabe. Ismay then commissioned a new line of steamships to compete on the transatlantic routes. The first of these, *Oceanic*, was delivered in 1871, to be followed by a staggering 49 others in the 44 years leading up to 1911. The fiftieth and fifty-first would be *Olympic* and *Titanic*.

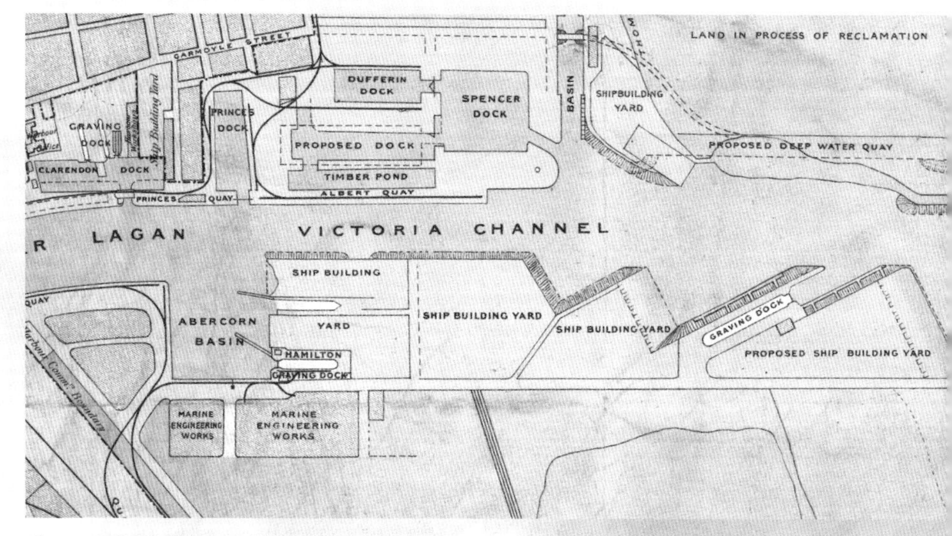

The map of 1872 (above left) foretells what was to come, with its dotted outlines indicating the proposed diagonal cuts that would create the North Yard slipways as they are today. This 1885 map shows the island's new saw-toothed configuration, which offered greater ship-launching capacity. The area of ground beneath the word 'Channel' on this map was destined to become the birthplace of the *Olympic*-class liners.

The Adriatic was the fifth steamship to be built by Harland & Wolff for the Oceanic Steam Navigation Company's new White Star Line. The sleek new passenger ships were all built with the flat 'Belfast bottom' hulls that Harland had pioneered, increasing both capacity and profitability.

PLAN OF
PART OF THE
PORT AND HARBOUR
OF
BELFAST.
W. REDFERN KELLY, M. INST. C.E. ENGINEER.
1912.
RECLAIMED LAND
MIDLAND RAILWAY COMPANY (NORTHERN COUNTIES COMMITTEE.)
TIMBER POND
TIMBER YARDS, &c.
DUFFERIN ROAD.
DUFFERIN DOCK
SPENCER DOCK
YORK DOCK
CLARENDON DOCK
SHIPBUILDING YARD
DONEGALL QUAY
ALBERT QUAY
VICTORIA CHANNEL
QUEEN'S QUAY
ABERCORN BASIN
VICTORIA WHARF
ALEXANDRA WHARF
NEW GRAVING DOCK
QUEEN'S ROAD
MARINE ENGINEERING WORKS
ALEXANDRA DOCK WORKS
PETROLEUM DEPOTS
MUSGRAVE CHANNEL
BUOYS
LAND RECLAIMED FROM THE SEA
CONNSWATER RIVER
VICTORIA PARK
BELFAST AND COUNTY DOWN RAILWAY COMPANY
RIVER LAGAN
CORPORATION STREET
YORK STREET
GARMOYLE ST.
NEWTOWNARDS ROAD
RAVENHILL ROAD
MAGNETIC NORTH
LATITUDE 54°-36'

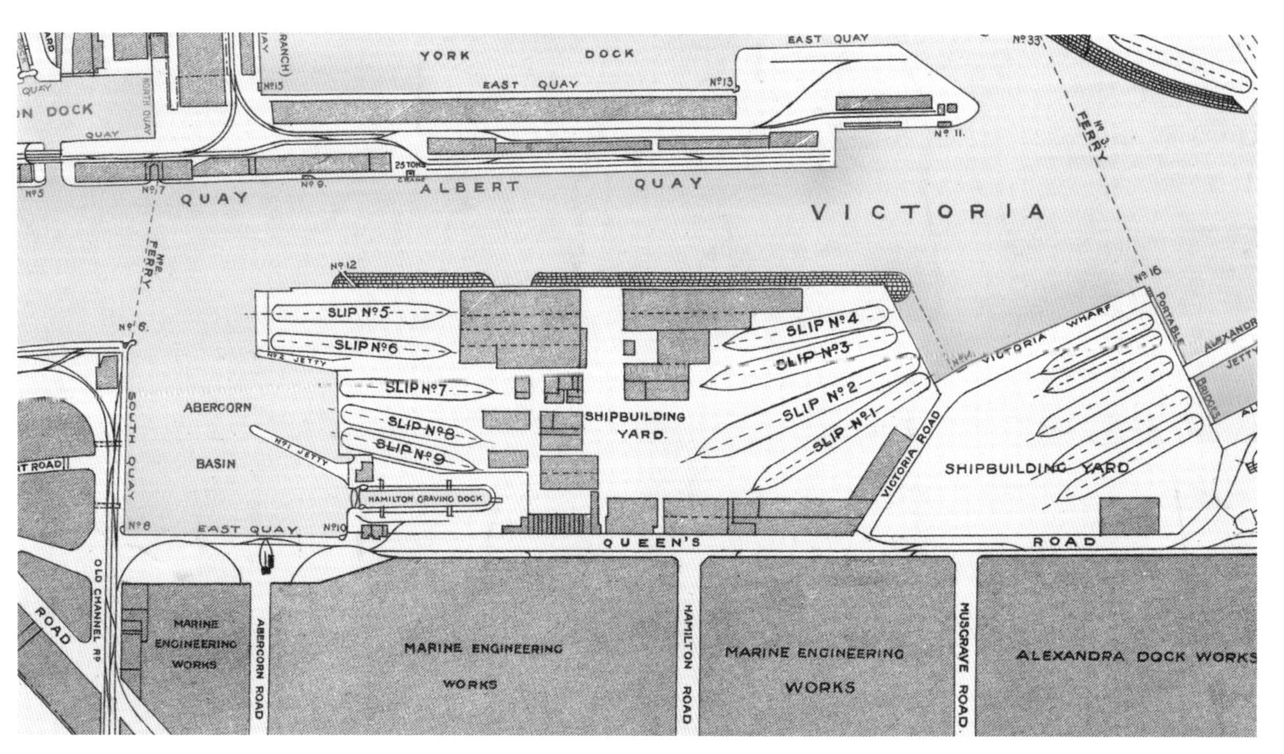

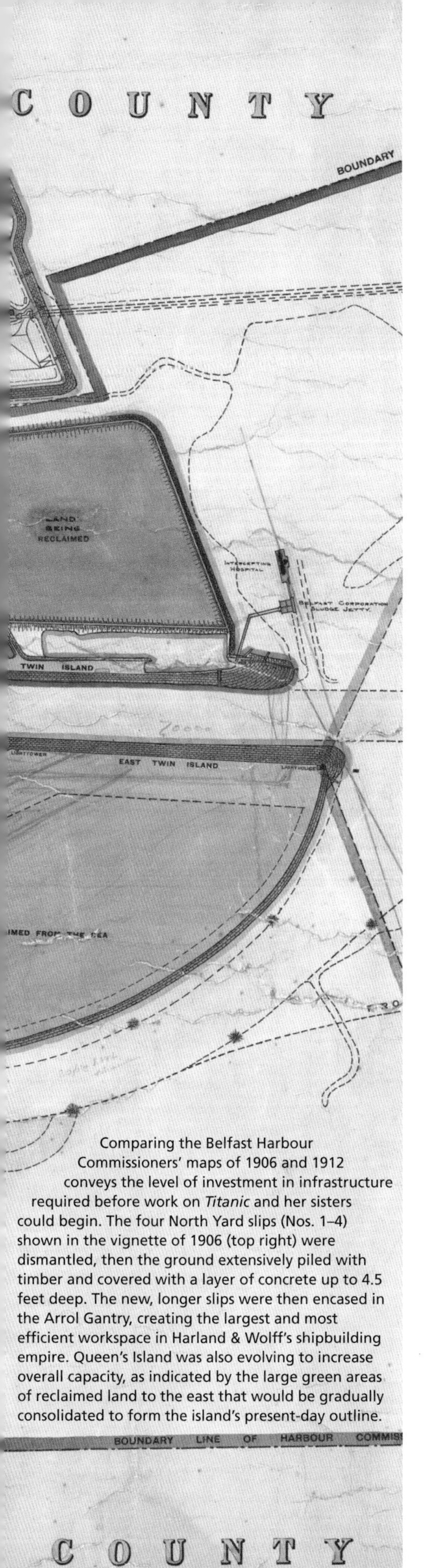

Comparing the Belfast Harbour Commissioners' maps of 1906 and 1912 conveys the level of investment in infrastructure required before work on *Titanic* and her sisters could begin. The four North Yard slips (Nos. 1–4) shown in the vignette of 1906 (top right) were dismantled, then the ground extensively piled with timber and covered with a layer of concrete up to 4.5 feet deep. The new, longer slips were then encased in the Arrol Gantry, creating the largest and most efficient workspace in Harland & Wolff's shipbuilding empire. Queen's Island was also evolving to increase overall capacity, as indicated by the large green areas of reclaimed land to the east that would be gradually consolidated to form the island's present-day outline.

Preparing for the giants

Like the land on which they stood, the shipyards of Queen's Island could be remoulded to suit the changing needs of industry. When the order for the *Olympic*-class liners was secured in early 1907, Harland & Wolff set about reorganising their operations to accommodate the scale of the White Star Line's ambitions. The North Yard's slips were reconfigured, reducing them from four to three. A parallel pair, each 990 feet long, now lay side by side within the new Arrol Gantry. Constructed by Sir William Arrol & Company of Glasgow at a cost of £100,000 (the equivalent of over £10 million today), the eponymous gantry was a prime example of Harland & Wolff's investment in the latest technology. Conventional steel shipbuilding at the time involved surprisingly low-tech temporary wooden staging across which framers, platers and riveters roamed. Multiple hoists were required to lift the steel plates into place; the length of their jibs dictated the extent of their reach, unless they were mounted on wheeled platforms. The more efficient Arrol Gantry created a permanent scaffold under which ships could be constructed, like caged animals awaiting release. The cranes and winches now ran on rails along the gantry's top, allowing them to deliver a plate to virtually any point along the hull. It also permitted much greater use of the latest hydraulic riveting machines, whose massive, vice-like jaws drove home the white-hot iron rivets to form joints of superior strength and reliability.

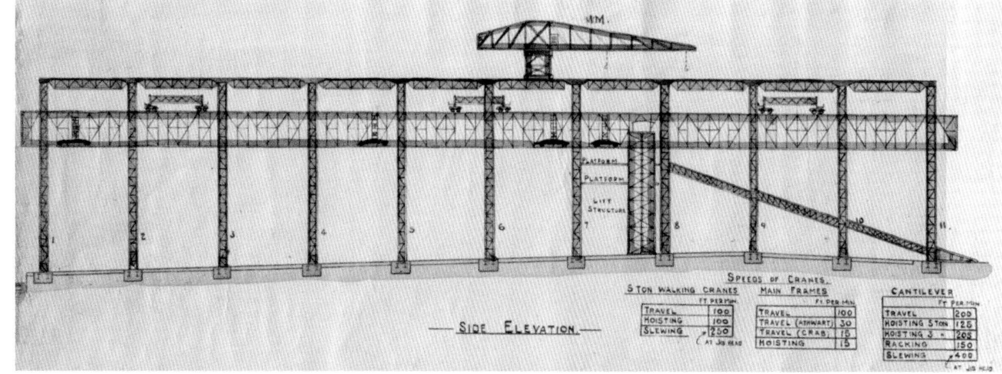

Measuring 228 feet in height from the ground to the top of its uppermost crane, the Arrol Gantry would come to dominate the Queen's Island skyline for decades. Arrol had made his name by constructing the world-famous Forth Bridge in Scotland in 1890, regarded as an engineering marvel even today. The gantry's cross-braced pylons clearly echo his main line of work.

Belfast born

The efficiency of the new gantry system can be gauged by the speed with which Harland & Wolff were able to construct the two largest moving objects the world had ever seen. The construction of the *Olympic*-class liners was deliberately staggered to reduce bottlenecks in the production of components, with *Olympic*'s keel being laid on 16th December 1908 and *Titanic*'s on 31st March 1909. Though she took four months longer to build than her older sister (whose hull was completed in just 22 months), *Titanic* was three inches longer. Those three inches secured for her the honour of being the largest ship afloat. Launched on 31st May 1911, her 882-foot, 9-inch hull slid smoothly down into the cold waters of the Victoria Channel, thanks to 15 tons of tallow, 3 tons of soft soap and a further 5 tons of tallow mixed with train oil. The largely empty hull was then moored beside the fitting-out wharf to receive its engines and superstructure.

Titanic remained in Belfast until her fit-out was completed on 31st March 1912, before venturing out for her sea trials on 2nd April. With the trials completed that same day, she left Belfast for the last time, heading off to Southampton to prepare for her maiden voyage. Just 13 days later, she would slide beneath the North Atlantic, not to be seen again until Dr Robert Ballard's camera picked her fractured hull out of the gloom on 2nd September 1987. Having spent three years and two days – almost 98 per cent of her short existence – on the Queen's Island slips or by its quays, no one could dispute Belfast's right to claim *Titanic* as her own.

Taken in May 1911, shortly before her launch, this archive image shows yard No. 401, *Titanic*, lying on No. 3 slip beneath the Arrol Gantry. Though still operating as a commercial vessel, the archaic wooden schooner in the foreground is a reminder of how far shipbuilding technology had advanced in under a hundred years.

The passing of the gantry

The Arrol Gantry had been state of the art when it was commissioned in 1908, but shipbuilding technology did not stand still. The advent of containerisation and the age of the supertanker after the Second World War spelled the end for the old ways. The new generation of vessels that appeared in the 1960s were simply too large to be launched in the traditional manner, requiring different facilities from those that the old yards had to offer. Switching their focus to the other side of Queen's Island, Harland & Wolff responded to these new challenges, creating the impressive modern Building Dock by enlarging a basin at the end of the Musgrave Channel (a southern spur of the Victoria Channel). Completed in 1970, the dock ushered in a new era in Belfast shipbuilding technology. From then on, the majority of vessels were prefabricated in large sections called 'super-blocks', then brought together by the giant yellow travelling gantry cranes Samson and Goliath for welding into a single unit. Ships no longer rose up from an inclined slipway to be slid dramatically into the waiting Lagan. Instead, the sluices of the dock were slowly opened and each new vessel was carefully floated off its keel blocks.

Floated out on 11th May 1970, the supertanker *Esso Ulidia* was the first ship to be constructed in Harland & Wolff's new Building Dock. Measuring 556 by 93 metres, this massive facility was one of the six largest dry docks in the world when it was built. Its two gantry cranes, Samson and Goliath, can both lift impressive loads of up to 840 tons each, as graphically illustrated by the this image of the *Esso Ulidia*'s upper superstructure being lowered into position.

There is a potent symbolism to this portrait of the Arrol Gantry taken in 1965, for the sun is setting behind a structure in the twilight of its career. Less than five years after it was taken, the steel silhouette that had dominated Belfast's skyline for over 60 years would be consigned to the scrap-heap.

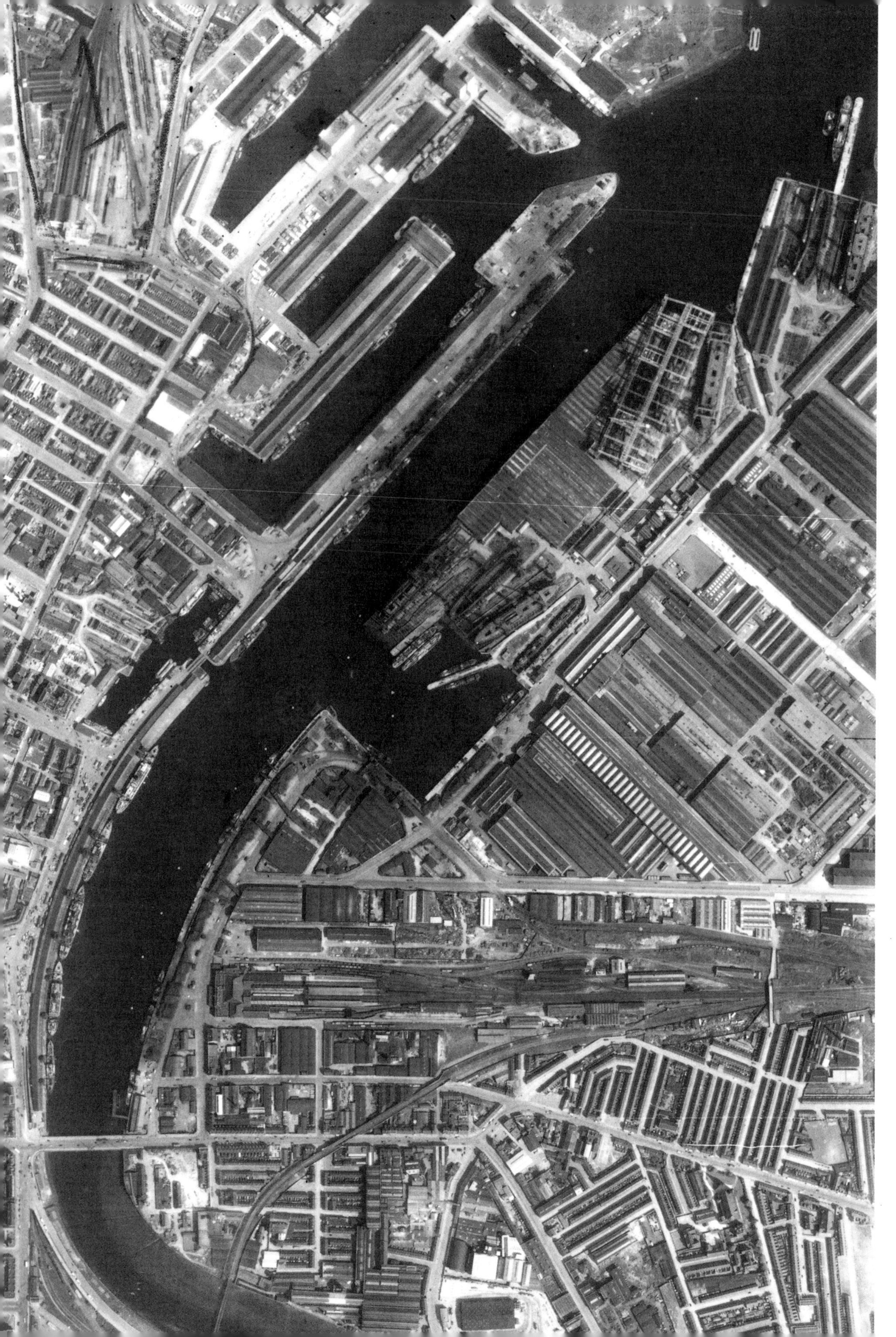

Post-industrial landscape

The last ship launched from the Queen's Yard (as the North Yard was by then known) was the *Leander*-class frigate HMS *Charybdis*, which left the No. 2 slipway on 28th February 1968. Once at the heart of Harland & Wolff's operations, the redundant Arrol Gantry was dismantled not long afterwards. Its stanchions were cut off at ground level and its 6,000 tons of steel sold for scrap. The inclined slipways it once embraced were filled in to serve as a staff car park and the activity of the yard that had forged the *Olympic*-class liners passed into memory.

Despite investing government loans in the advanced Building Dock, Harland & Wolff's future was by no means secure. The whole UK shipbuilding industry had been suffering severe decline for decades, thanks to the combined effects of soaring costs, long-running industrial disputes and increased competition from cheaper labour forces overseas, particularly in South Korea. In 1977 the British government decided to nationalise the UK's ailing shipyards. While many of its old competitors would be wound up, Harland & Wolff survived. The firm returned to private hands in 1989, when it became the subject of a management/staff buyout, led by the Norwegian firm of Fred. Olsen Energy. The business was bought back from the UK government to become Harland & Wolff Holdings plc.

Part of the RAF's post-war aerial survey of Northern Ireland, this photograph, taken on 17th May 1952, shows Queen's Island at its industrial peak. The North and South Yards are busy, with at least half of the slipways occupied by hulls at various stages of construction. Fanning out along the reclaimed peninsula, Harland & Wolff's extensive operation was an industrial city within a city.

A new quarter for Belfast

The name upon the gates may have changed little, but the company behind them was a fraction of its former size. From its post-Second World War peak of some 35,000 employees, Harland & Wolff Holdings now had a workforce of only 3,000 and it was still falling. The decrease in business and the land needed to service it led the shipbuilding operation to contract, and by the 1990s a large swathe of Queen's Island lay silent.

Seeking to replicate its parent company's success in creating business parks on post-industrial sites, Fred. Olsen Energy began separating the assets of Harland & Wolff Holdings into land and shipping. In 1990 Harland & Wolff Properties Ltd was formed to oversee any commercial redevelopment. As the land bank grew ever larger, however, it became clear that this was potentially far more than a business park. By redeveloping roughly a hundred acres of redundant land, they could create a whole new part of Belfast. In 1998 this ideological shift led to the formation of two subsidiary companies, Titanic Properties Ltd and Titanic Quarter Ltd, and in December 2000 the latter reached a pivotal deal with the landowners, the Belfast Harbour Commissioners. The Titanic Quarter Master Agreement created a 30-year window in which the old yards could be redeveloped, with the commissioners as co-promoters of the scheme.

Fifty years after the RAF's Spitfires had recorded a hive of heavy industry, this aerial photograph, taken *c.* 2002, shows a landscape transformed. The gantries, sheds and slipways of the North and South Yards were no more, and Queen's Island now resembled a concrete aircraft carrier, moored near Belfast's heart. The gold outline of Titanic Quarter's land bank illustrates the scale of the opportunity this post-industrial waterfront now presented.

This view down the crumbling concrete edges of *Titanic*'s No. 3 slip shows how much imagination was required to mentally transform this derelict shipyard into a thriving new quarter for Belfast.

Designs on Queen's Island

In 2001 Fred. Olsen Energy began separating its industrial and development assets to allow it to concentrate on its core activities in oil, gas and shipping. It placed both Titanic Quarter Ltd and Titanic Properties Ltd under the umbrella of a new company, Ivy Wood Properties, which included the development rights to the Queen's Island land, negotiated the year before. In 2002 Titanic Quarter Ltd and the Belfast Harbour Commissioners jointly commissioned Turley Associates to produce the *Development Framework Document*, exploring the future shape of the new Titanic Quarter. The diagrammatic masterplans in that document sought to replicate the scale and urban grain of Belfast's historic city centre, dividing the land into a mixed-use grid of garden squares. The future use of the historic slipways was left open, encouraging potential partners, such as Museums and Galleries of Northern Ireland (MAGNI), to consider creating cultural components to enhance Titanic Quarter's appeal. By mid-2003 MAGNI had commissioned its own feasibility study into founding a new museum on or around the *Titanic* and *Olympic* slips, which confirmed that the location held great potential. However, MAGNI were subsequently granted substantial public funds to refurbish their existing sites, effectively ruling out any relocation to the slipways.

The sale of Ivy Wood Properties in 2004 came complete with the initial plans for Titanic Quarter, but it would take an immense collective effort to begin to turn these into reality. Pat Doherty (centre) is pictured here on a tour of the slipways with Conal Harvey (left), the Director of Operations at Harcourt Developments, and Frank Cushnahan CBE (right), Chairman of the Belfast Harbour Commissioners.

It was at this moment that one of Ireland's most successful property developers, Pat Doherty, Chairman of Harcourt Developments, visited the nascent Titanic Quarter. Standing on the slipways in 2003, he was immediately struck by their unique potential. As Doherty himself observed, 'It's not often that a site of nearly 200 acres comes up in the middle of a city.' He persuaded renowned Irish businessman and financier Dermot Desmond to jointly invest in Queen's Island and together they bought Ivy Wood Properties from Fred. Olsen Energy. The official transfer of the lease to Pat Doherty's Harcourt Developments in February 2004 was to be a defining moment, for he and his Harcourt team, led by Conal Harvey, would provide much of the driving force behind Titanic Belfast.

A team assembles

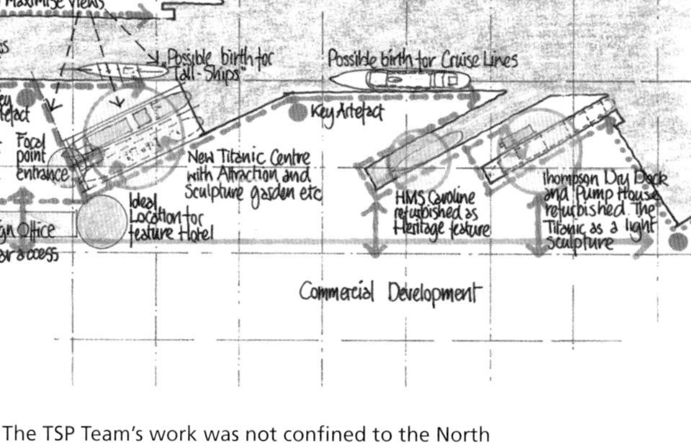

We can now return to where this chapter began, for the parallel stories of Queen's Island and Titanic Belfast converged in 2004. While Titanic Quarter Ltd was being transferred to Harcourt Developments, an independent group of mainly public-sector institutions had been exploring the role *Titanic* might play in Belfast's future. In 2001 these institutions had established the Titanic Forum, which was comprised of a number of like-minded local bodies interested in preserving and promoting the history and heritage of Belfast's docks and shipyards. It included Belfast City Council, NITB, the Arts Council of Northern Ireland, Belfast Industrial Heritage Ltd, Titanic Quarter Ltd, the Department of Culture, Arts and Leisure and the Department of Enterprise, Trade and Investment. All agreed that options for a high-profile 'Titanic Signature Project' should be investigated in greater detail, to determine what economic and cultural benefits it might bring to the city.

The TSP Team's work was not confined to the North Yard. The historic slipways were just one component of the '*Titanic* Trail' of maritime monuments, including the Thompson Graving Dock and HMS *Caroline*, the last surviving ship from the Battle of Jutland. The team explored ways of threading these landmarks together to create a vibrant 'heritage spine' for Queen's Island, with the Titanic Signature Project as its centrepiece.

In early 2004 NITB duly issued their *Strategic Framework for Action 2004–2007*, complete with their list of five potential Signature Projects that included the *Titanic* (maritime)/Belfast theme. In June that year the Titanic Forum, acting through Belfast City Council, put out a tender to study the feasibility of a Titanic Signature Project. The tender was won by a group assembled by Michael Counahan of CHL Consulting, a specialist destination-development, management and research consultancy based in Dublin. Counahan's team included economic-development consultants Colin Stutt, property management experts GVA Grimley, and exhibition designers Event Communications. This was the original Titanic Signature Project Team (TSP Team). Its key personnel, including Counahan himself, would stay with the project for the duration, seeing it all the way through to completion in 2012 and beyond. The inclusion of Event, Europe's leading exhibition-design group, was an indication of the level of expectation that surrounded the *Titanic* concept from the outset. Buoyed by *Titanic*'s international recognition factor, this was a concept with the potential to become Belfast's twenty-first century signature.

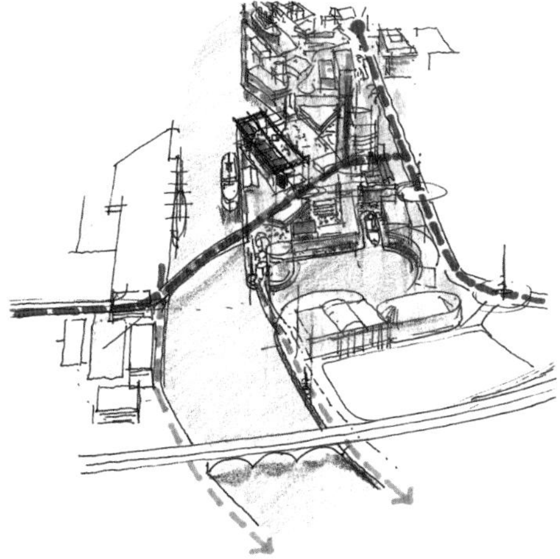

Possible 'tramway' link: linking the Titanic slipway with the City Centre, Cathedral Quarter, Laganside and the Odyssey

Conveying the scale of *Titanic* without resorting to a direct facsimile, Event's concept of a 'Ghost Ship' returned to port caught the imagination of many in the Titanic Forum. Translating the lines of the hull and superstructure into a cage of LED strips, the Ghost Ship would have created a landmark without obscuring the fabric of the historic Thompson Graving Dock it occupied. Begun well before the Arrol Gantry, the impressive graving dock was completed just in time for the fitting out of the *Olympic* in 1911.

Hulls and gantries

The TSP Team began work in late 2004, building a detailed list of desirable elements that would meet the expectations of an international audience. The report mapped out the scope and components for the project, including a central exhibition, a banqueting suite, a shop, restaurants and a temporary gallery. All of these would find their way into Titanic Belfast. Taking a holistic view of Titanic Quarter and its existing heritage assets, they considered several different locations for the main attraction, including the old Harland & Wolff headquarters. Ultimately, it was the long expanse of the North Yard's slipways, with their direct connection to *Titanic*'s construction, that remained the most compelling option. CHL engaged Murray Ó Laoire Architects (MÓLA) to investigate the possible architecture of the attraction.

MÓLA's concept proposals focused on the form of the Arrol Gantry and the relationship between its rigid frame of girders and the more organic, graceful hulls that once grew within it. By inserting virtual models of *Olympic* and *Titanic* between the lines of pylons, then slowly subtracting and subdividing their volumes to house different functions, the team created an abstract composition of interconnected pavilions that flowed around the slipways as the narrative unfolded. Event Communications painted a compelling vision for recreating the working shipyard within the gantry frames, using large-scale models of partly fabricated hulls to portray Edwardian shipbuilding techniques. The team quickly realised that the sheer scale of the slipways made the gantry concept uneconomical, for the footprint of the gantry produced a volume that far exceeded the space requirements of the desired components.

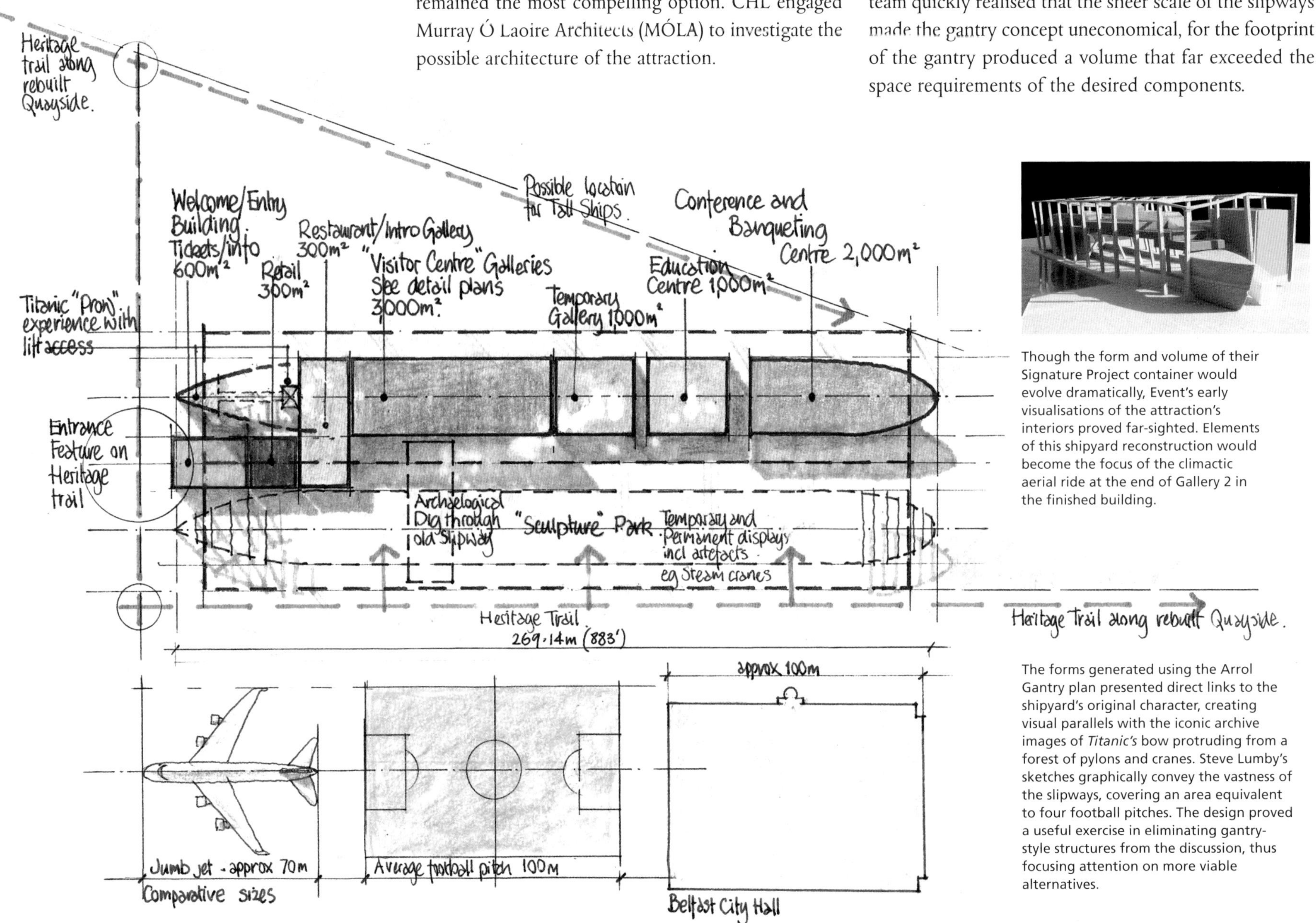

Though the form and volume of their Signature Project container would evolve dramatically, Event's early visualisations of the attraction's interiors proved far-sighted. Elements of this shipyard reconstruction would become the focus of the climactic aerial ride at the end of Gallery 2 in the finished building.

The forms generated using the Arrol Gantry plan presented direct links to the shipyard's original character, creating visual parallels with the iconic archive images of *Titanic's* bow protruding from a forest of pylons and cranes. Steve Lumby's sketches graphically convey the vastness of the slipways, covering an area equivalent to four football pitches. The design proved a useful exercise in eliminating gantry-style structures from the discussion, thus focusing attention on more viable alternatives.

Dividing a quarter

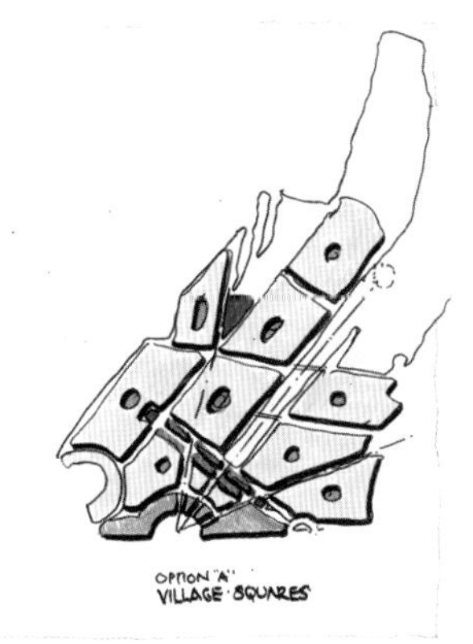

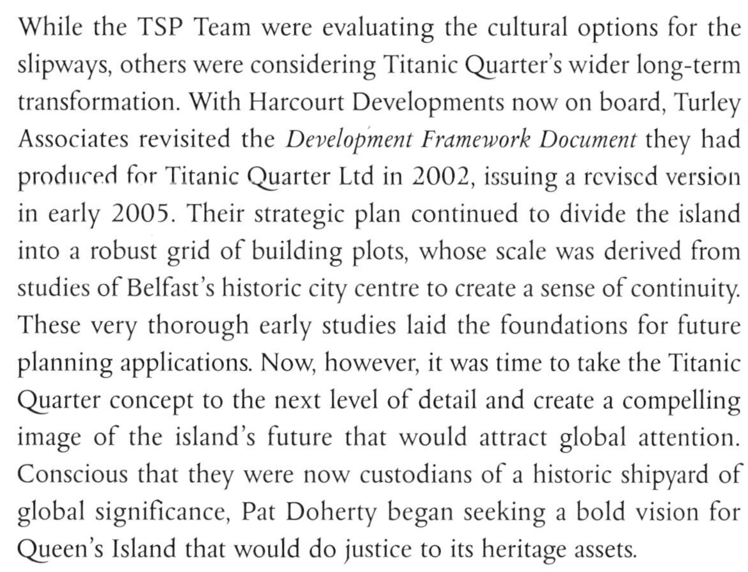

While the TSP Team were evaluating the cultural options for the slipways, others were considering Titanic Quarter's wider long-term transformation. With Harcourt Developments now on board, Turley Associates revisited the *Development Framework Document* they had produced for Titanic Quarter Ltd in 2002, issuing a revised version in early 2005. Their strategic plan continued to divide the island into a robust grid of building plots, whose scale was derived from studies of Belfast's historic city centre to create a sense of continuity. These very thorough early studies laid the foundations for future planning applications. Now, however, it was time to take the Titanic Quarter concept to the next level of detail and create a compelling image of the island's future that would attract global attention. Conscious that they were now custodians of a historic shipyard of global significance, Pat Doherty began seeking a bold vision for Queen's Island that would do justice to its heritage assets.

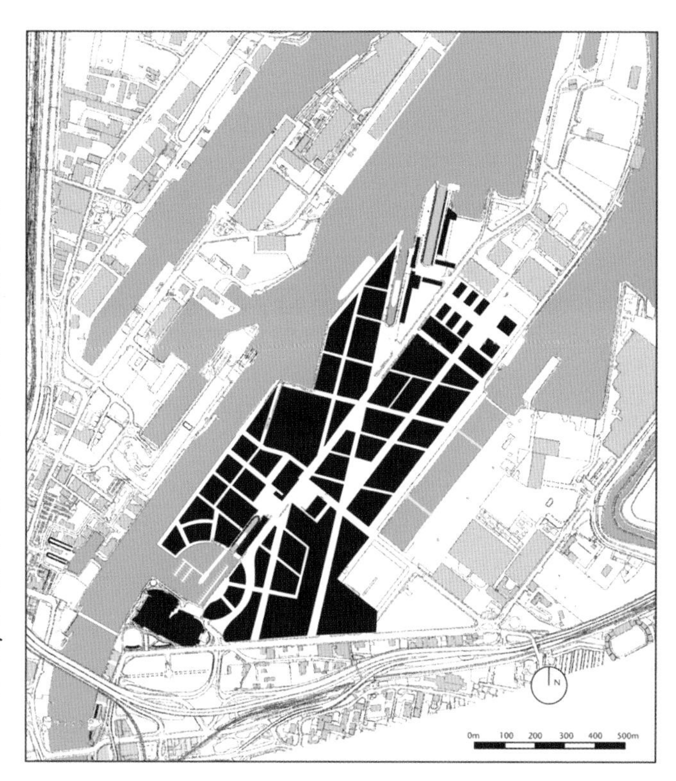

One of the crucial differences between Turley's *Development Framework Document* (above) and CivicArts's Titanic Quarter Vision Plan (below) was the widening of the brief to include areas of active industrial land that were outside of Titanic Quarter Ltd's control. The intention was not to pre-empt the end of heavy engineering on the island, but to allow for the coherent future expansion of the street grid if the land should become vacant at a later date. This future-proofing strategy ensured that graceful sightlines and circulation would be preserved.

Ironically, it would be work on another island that brought Pat Doherty into contact with architect and masterplanner Eric R. Kuhne. Both men were independently involved in work on St Helier, Jersey, with Kuhne busy designing the mixed-use waterfront at Castle Quay while Doherty redeveloped Liberty Wharf. Doherty mentioned his desire to find a vision for Titanic Quarter to David Margason, Managing Director of Jersey's Waterfront Enterprise Board, who immediately recommended Kuhne. Meeting at the London offices of Kuhne's practice, CivicArts, in January 2005, the Donegal developer and the Texan architect quickly established a great personal rapport. Rolling out one of many concept designs then circulating for Titanic Quarter, Doherty invited Kuhne to offer his opinion and suggest how he might approach the masterplan. This informal meeting would prove to be a turning point, not only in the evolution of Titanic Quarter but also in the creation of Titanic Belfast.

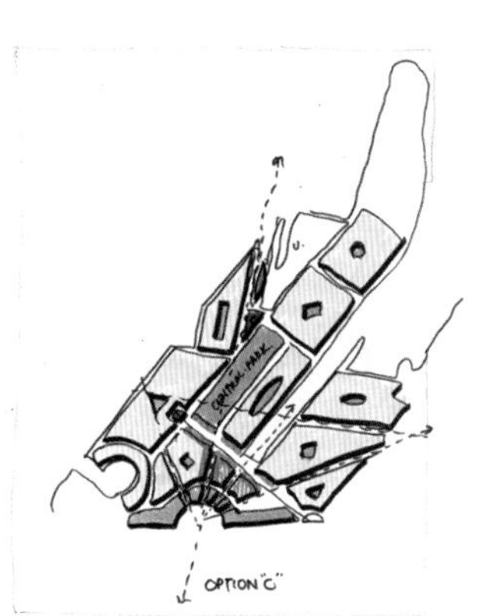

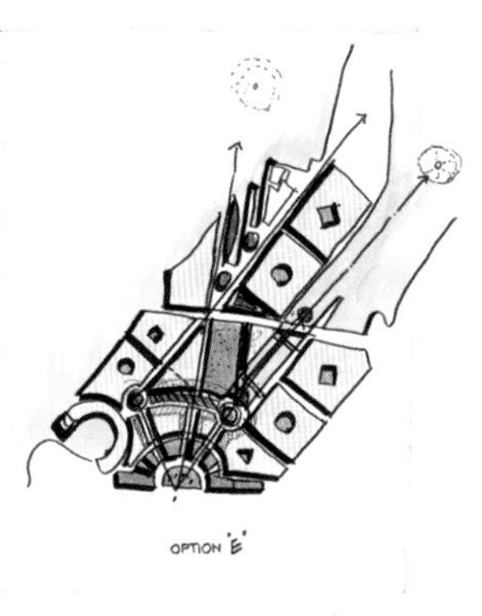

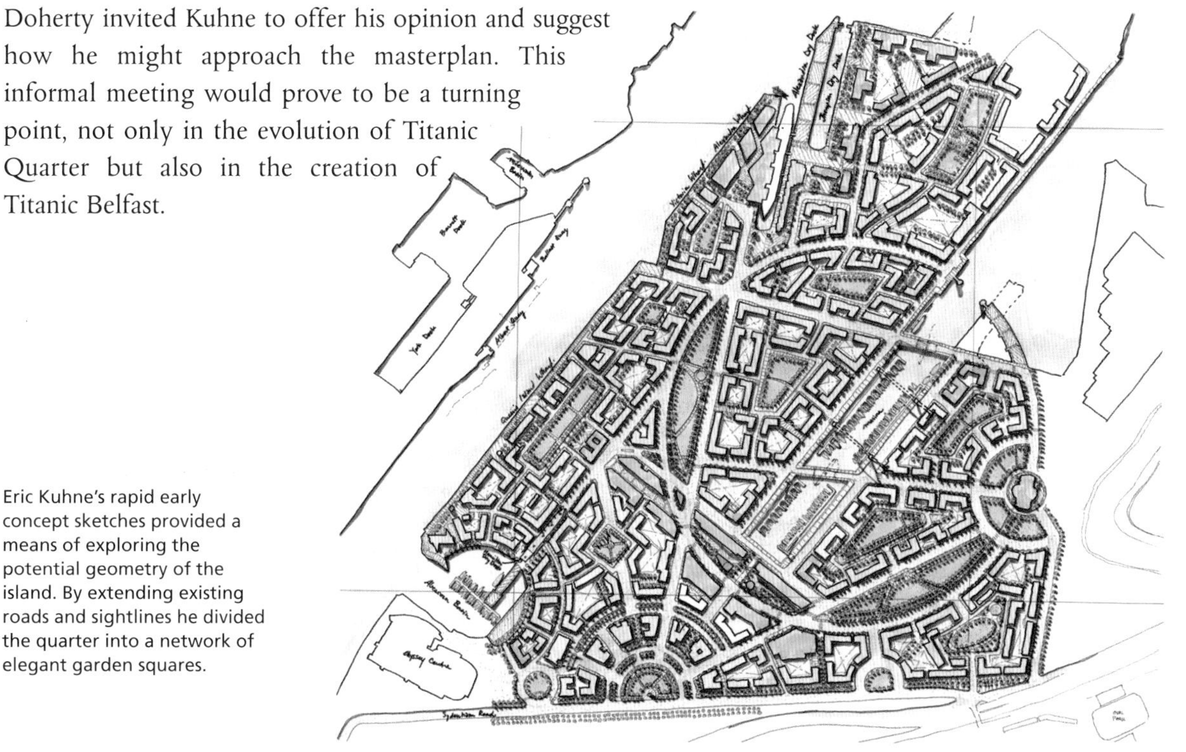

Eric Kuhne's rapid early concept sketches provided a means of exploring the potential geometry of the island. By extending existing roads and sightlines he divided the quarter into a network of elegant garden squares.

A new vision for Titanic Quarter

People would be at the heart of Kuhne's new vision for Titanic Quarter. The population of Belfast had been in decline for decades, plummeting from a mid-twentieth-century peak of 400,000 to around 270,000 in the early 2000s. The violence of the Troubles had certainly contributed to this great exodus, but rising crime and industrial decline were also significant contributors. Kuhne made the crucial observation that if Titanic Quarter were to thrive it would have to halt the mass migration of citizens to the surrounding countryside. Following his initial meeting with Pat Doherty, Kuhne wasted no time in visiting Belfast himself. Together with his long time colleague, David Beale, he set off on a tour of the outlying hamlets, towns and fishing villages. Everywhere the pair went, they asked people the same simple question: 'What would it take to get you to move back to Belfast?' The answer came back loud and clear. People wanted the city to provide what these villages offered them: fresh air, comfortable homes, safe streets and local services. Kuhne's challenge was to combine that rural sense of community and security with the convenience of urban amenities and employment, uniting them to form a model of sustainable modern living.

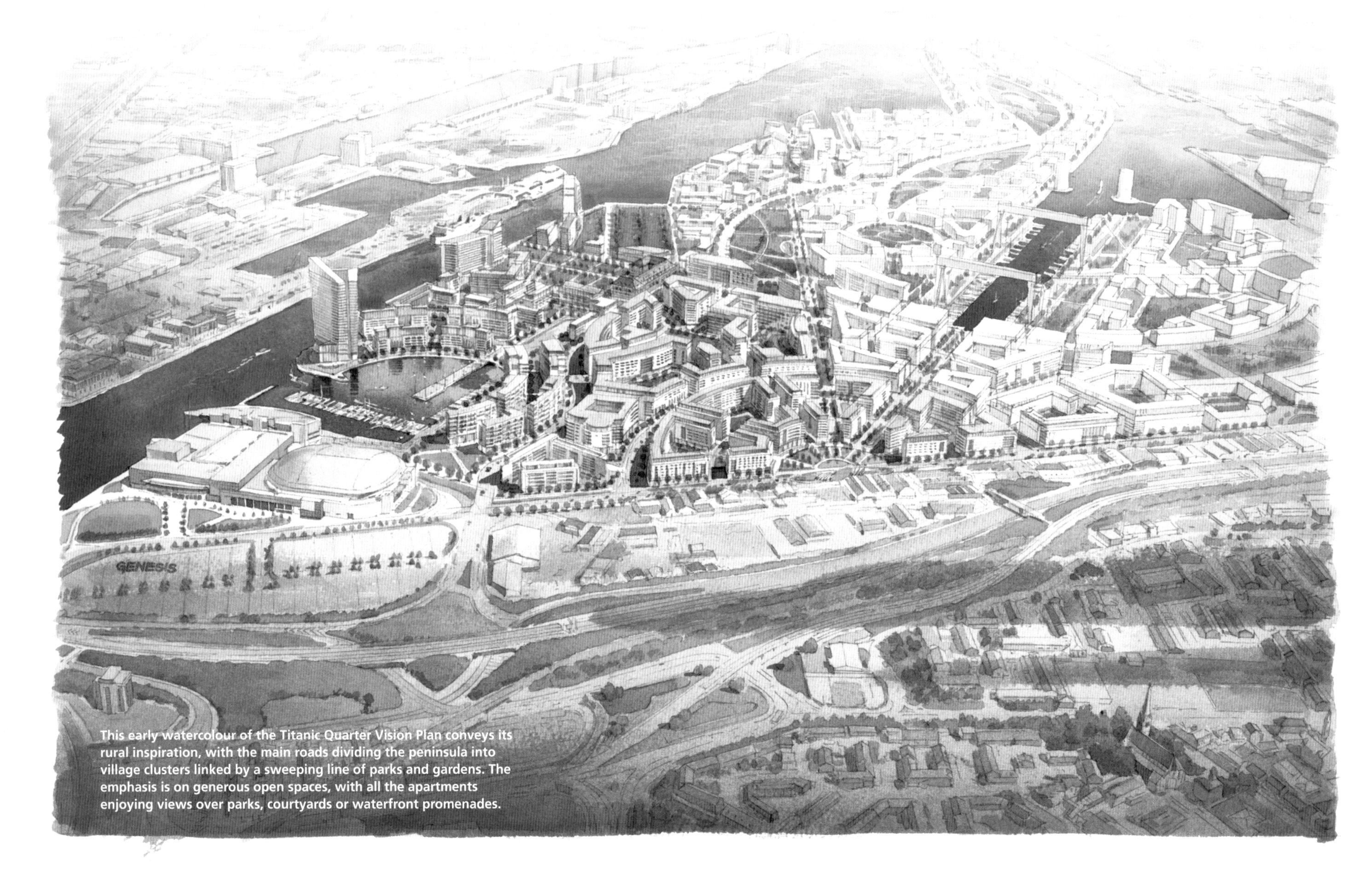

This early watercolour of the Titanic Quarter Vision Plan conveys its rural inspiration, with the main roads dividing the peninsula into village clusters linked by a sweeping line of parks and gardens. The emphasis is on generous open spaces, with all the apartments enjoying views over parks, courtyards or waterfront promenades.

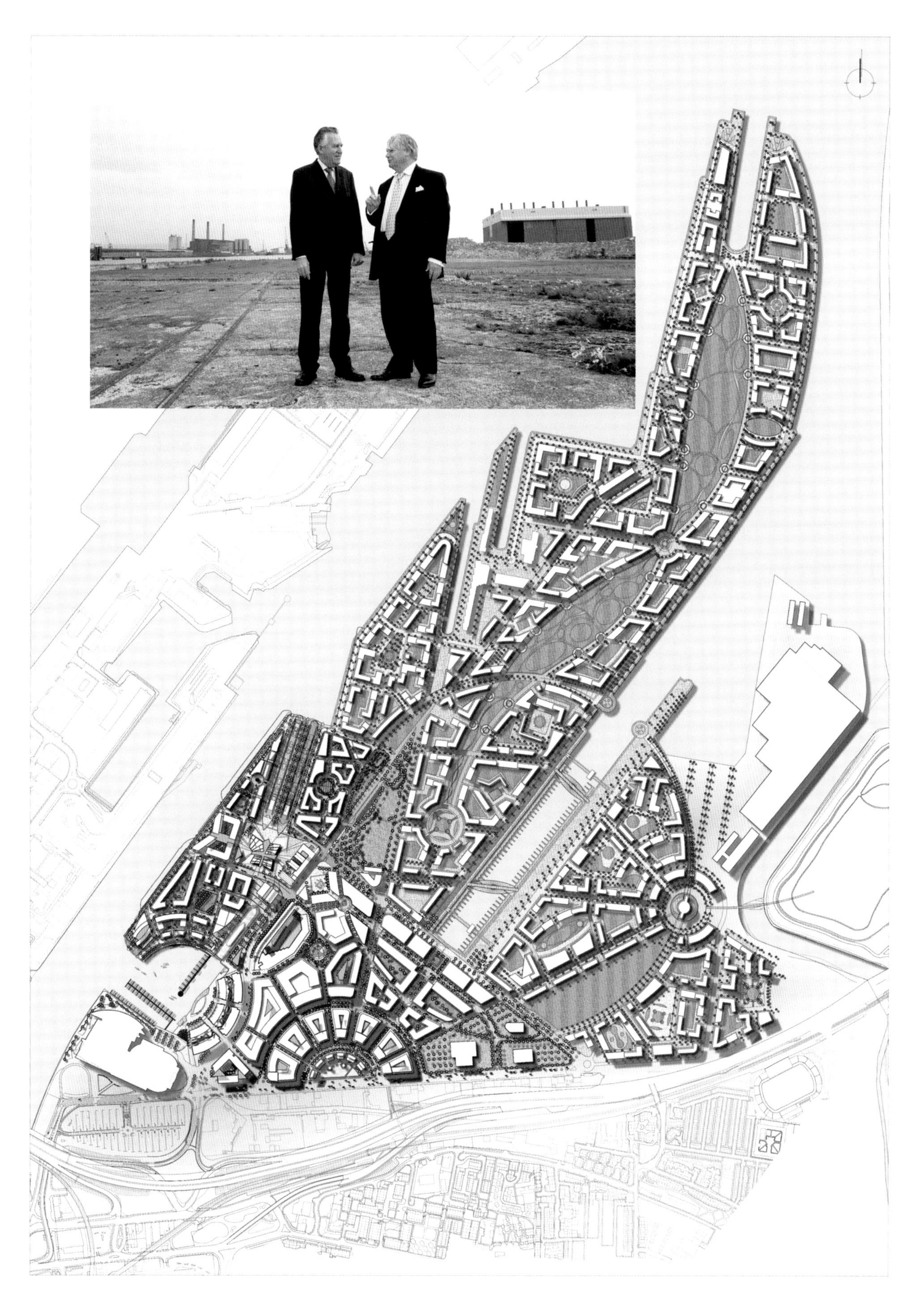

Dignitaries attending the official launch of the Titanic Quarter Vision Plan on 18th October 2005 were given a preliminary guided tour of the historic slipways. Standing amidst the barren expanse of concrete and rubble, Pat Doherty (now Chairman of Titanic Quarter Ltd.) converses with Peter Hain, then Secretary of State for Northern Ireland, discussing his vision for transforming Queen's Island.

Just as the new Vision Plan was taking shape, the work of the TSP Team was coming to a close. Belfast City Council signed off on the team's final report in June 2005, but Pat Doherty and his colleague Conal Harvey were quick to recognise the importance of both the Signature Project concept and the research done to date. Their prompt decision to re-engage CHL and its team as consultants to Titanic Quarter preserved their accumulated knowledge base and maintained vital momentum on the project. The proposed content of the attraction was clearly sound, but its outward form and location still had to be determined. The most pressing question was how such a major cultural attraction might be successfully integrated into the broader vision for the new quarter. Kuhne would later recall how Doherty casually broached the subject in the echoing marble corridors of Belfast City Hall, following another review of the emerging masterplan: perhaps he would also like to review some existing proposals for a Titanic Signature Project on the slipways? The road to Titanic Belfast lay open.

Though heavily refined, the current Titanic Quarter Vision Plan has remained true to the early designs laid out by CivicArts over the summer of 2005. The lyrical forms of the ribbon parks linked eight distinct residential villages, interspersed with vital amenities and centres of employment. This deliberate layering of uses included public and civic spaces such as the slipway parks and waterfront promenades.

The concept plan extended beyond the boundaries of Titanic Quarter to encompass active industrial areas, thus ensuring that any future developments could be seamlessly integrated if the land should become vacant. Combining CivicArts's vision with Turley's local knowledge and expertise, the initial phases of the new Titanic Quarter were successfully submitted for planning, with some 30 separate developments being approved by the end of 2012.

Designing an icon

How do you design an icon? This was the challenge posed by Pat Doherty when he invited CivicArts to submit their ideas on the Signature Project late in the summer of 2005. The answer lay in defining what this icon was to represent, for if it was to be a genuine symbol for Belfast and Northern Ireland it needed to say something meaningful about the industry that once held sway on this armature of reclaimed land. It was clear that this could not be a monument only to one ship, but rather to all ships and to the workforce that designed and built them. It must acknowledge the tragedy, certainly, but also celebrate the triumph of engineering that continued long after *Titanic* had steamed out of Belfast Lough and met her fate in the North Atlantic. This was not to be a case of wishful revisionism, but a voyage of rediscovery, throwing the spotlight on a proud past that had long lain neglected and bringing Belfast out of the shadow of the great disaster to recognise its proud legacy in this field of industry.

Drawn retrospectively, Eric Kuhne's sketch evolution of Titanic Belfast illustrates how the essential composition of a cluster of hard, jagged forms has remained constant throughout the whole process.

Why not build a new *Titanic*?

Pat Doherty's choice of concept architect was well informed, for Eric Kuhne and his colleagues at CivicArts could boast a long track record of site-specific projects across the world. Wherever the project, from the Kentish countryside to Sydney's waterfront, their work consistently responded to the history, culture and ethos of the setting. Actively celebrating the narrative qualities of architecture, CivicArts's working method placed an emphasis on preliminary cultural research. By immersing themselves in the rich history of Queen's Island and industrial Belfast, they found an abundance of possible precedents to apply to the brief in hand.

Architect Eric R. Kuhne at work in his office. Sketching and hand drawing remain core skills at CivicArts, where many options are explored in quick succession in the search for forms that convey the strongest narrative.

The enduring popularity of *Titanic* and her story can be gauged by the diversity of ideas that were already in circulation when CivicArts became involved in 2005. A public advertisement placed by Belfast City Council and NITB inviting suggestions for the Signature Project proved very popular. One recurring idea was a reproduction of the ship herself, varying from scaled-down partial models on shore to full-sized sailing replicas.

A wealthy overseas businessman had reportedly approached Harland & Wolff back in the 1990s, enquiring about the cost of producing three modern reproductions of *Titanic* – but this, along with many similar schemes, had foundered on grounds of practicality and cost. The essential problem with building a replica Edwardian liner in the twenty-first century was that shipbuilding had moved on in quantum leaps. What had been a state of-the-art ship in 1912 would not have a hope of meeting the stringent safety standards required of modern cruise ships, unless its internal arrangements were radically reorganised. And, if the ship could not be an exact replica, what true value would it have?

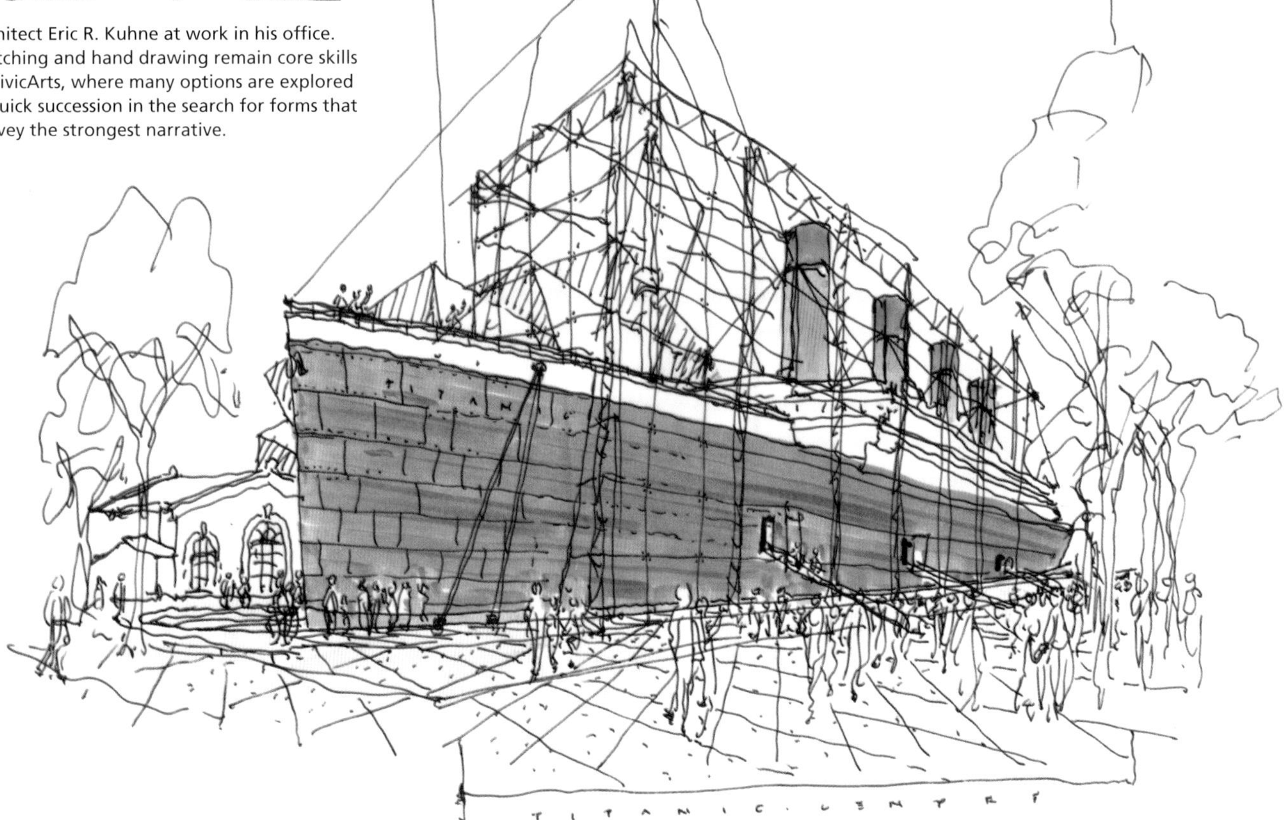

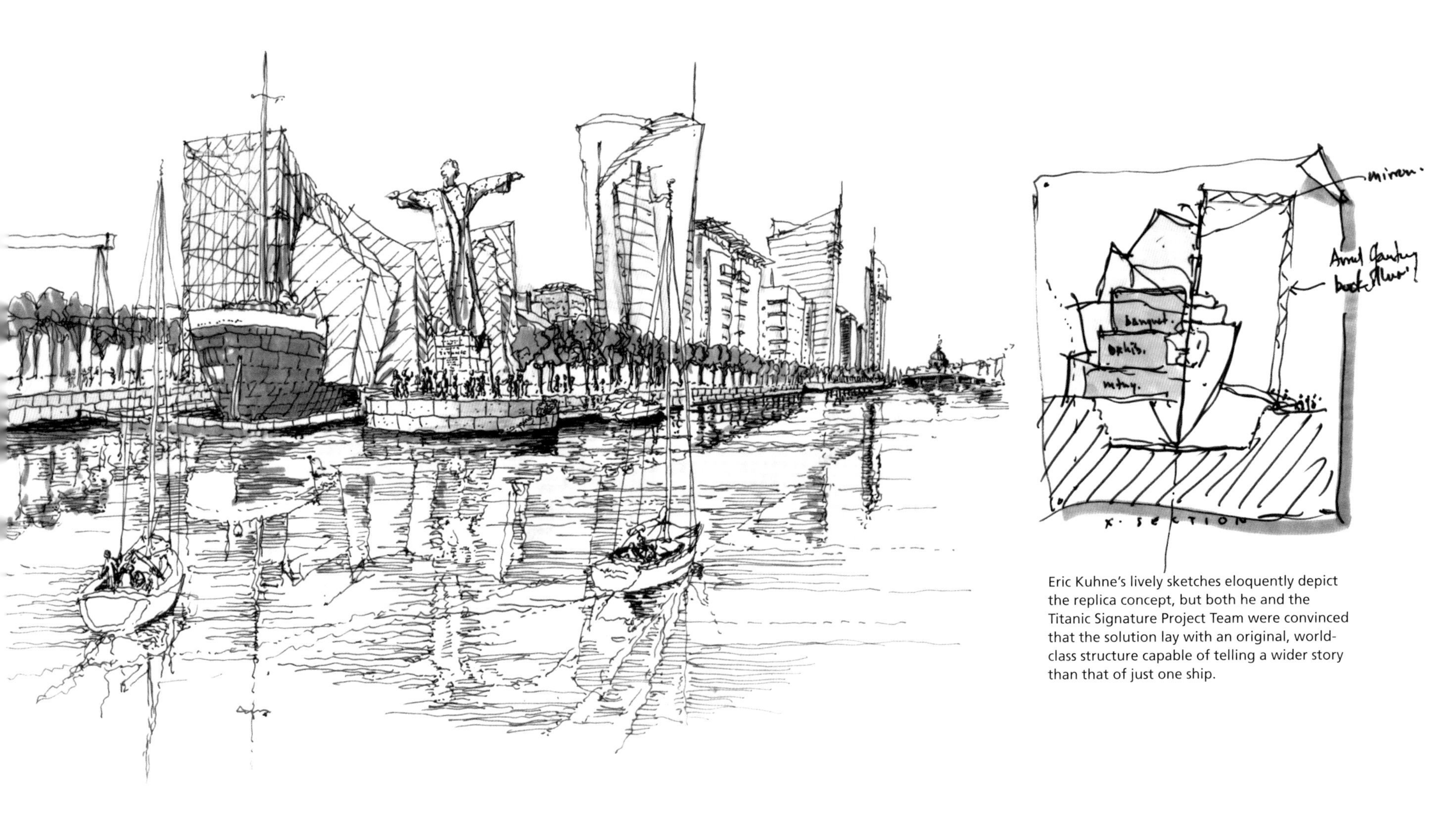

Eric Kuhne's lively sketches eloquently depict the replica concept, but both he and the Titanic Signature Project Team were convinced that the solution lay with an original, world-class structure capable of telling a wider story than that of just one ship.

Despite these considerations, the concept of some form of replica persisted, with some prominent people as supporters, so CivicArts were asked to explore the feasibility of incorporating some portion of *Titanic* into the design. Given that *Titanic* was launched from the slipways before her superstructure was built, the idea of placing a complete replica on this site was anathema to the design team, so the Thompson Graving Dock was selected as a possible location. Recognising that the confines of a complete hull were incompatible with the activities the attraction would have to support, Kuhne's exploratory sketches envisaged a building of two halves, with one elevation presenting a full-sized facsimile of the ship resting on the dock floor, supported by elements derived from the Arrol Gantry. On the opposite side, a series of large exhibition, conference and banqueting spaces would span the gap between dock and ship – all stacked within a unifying glass envelope whose jagged panes would resemble an iceberg.

Comparing the scale silhouettes of the Edwardian *Titanic* and the modern *Queen Mary II* graphically conveys how the cruise ships of today dwarf their famous predecessors.

Drawn to provoke debate, the sketches succeeded in convincing most commentators that the replica route would not result in the quality landmark Belfast deserved. Given the quantity of genuine industrial heritage in the immediate area, a facsimile of the ship ran the real risk of producing a theme-park-style 'Disneyfication' of what had been a hard and gritty enterprise. It would also serve as a reminder that, although *Titanic* was famed for her size when launched, she was surpassed in scale within a matter of months by the launch of the German-built *Bismarck* in June 1914. Bismarck was over 73 feet longer than *Titanic*, while Cunard's famous *Queen Mary* – launched in 1934 – was 137 feet longer. Her modern successor, the gigantic *Queen Mary II*, is a staggering 250 feet longer than *Titanic*, with nearly three times her displacement. To build a full-sized replica revealing the old liner's true scale might well diminish the great ship and undermine the legend. Though physically overshadowed by her successors, *Titanic* looms largest in the imagination.

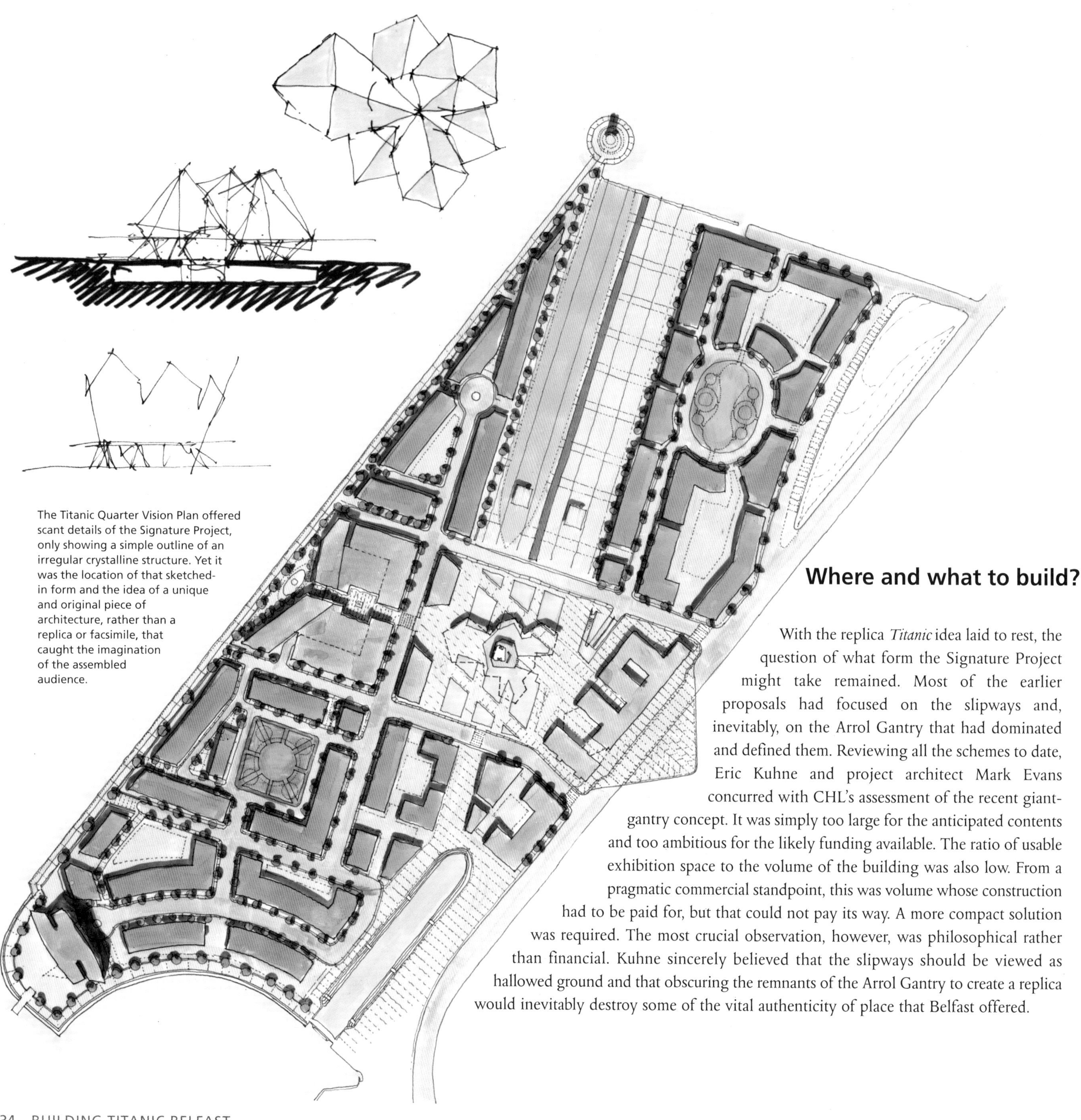

The Titanic Quarter Vision Plan offered scant details of the Signature Project, only showing a simple outline of an irregular crystalline structure. Yet it was the location of that sketched-in form and the idea of a unique and original piece of architecture, rather than a replica or facsimile, that caught the imagination of the assembled audience.

Where and what to build?

With the replica *Titanic* idea laid to rest, the question of what form the Signature Project might take remained. Most of the earlier proposals had focused on the slipways and, inevitably, on the Arrol Gantry that had dominated and defined them. Reviewing all the schemes to date, Eric Kuhne and project architect Mark Evans concurred with CHL's assessment of the recent giant-gantry concept. It was simply too large for the anticipated contents and too ambitious for the likely funding available. The ratio of usable exhibition space to the volume of the building was also low. From a pragmatic commercial standpoint, this was volume whose construction had to be paid for, but that could not pay its way. A more compact solution was required. The most crucial observation, however, was philosophical rather than financial. Kuhne sincerely believed that the slipways should be viewed as hallowed ground and that obscuring the remnants of the Arrol Gantry to create a replica would inevitably destroy some of the vital authenticity of place that Belfast offered.

A literal interpretation of a historic precedent, the early clustered 'Crystal Palace' concepts were derived from the faceted forms of quartz. These studies gave rise to a fractured, irregular solid that replaced the conventional memorial originally envisaged as the centrepiece of the water garden beside the drawing offices.

Searching for alternative narratives, the team looked back in time to Queen's Island's first Victorian incarnation as the People's Park. Central to that public pleasure-ground had been the sparkling Crystal Palace, whose exotic plants, animals and curiosities had delighted visitors until its tragic loss to fire in 1864. With the high ratio of green spaces now being proposed for Queen's Island's post-industrial landscape, this seemed a highly appropriate precedent. In the course of evolving the Titanic Quarter Vision Plan, CivicArts had already pencilled in a formal water garden at the head of the slipways as part of the landscaping around the former Harland & Wolff headquarters building. The public launch of the Vision Plan was due to take place on 18th October 2005, in the very drawing offices where *Titanic* had been designed. Just a few days before the launch, the simple outline of a faceted structure was sketched in the midst of the water garden, straddling the intersecting sightlines of the slipways and the drawing offices. The idea had crystallised. In his keynote address that night, Kuhne's use of the phrase 'hallowed ground' found deep resonance amongst many of the heritage bodies and local-interest groups present. The idea of building a totally original structure at the slipways' head took hold. The crystal outline, and the crucial move away from the slipways themselves, were to make this presentation one of the defining moments in the evolution of Titanic Belfast.

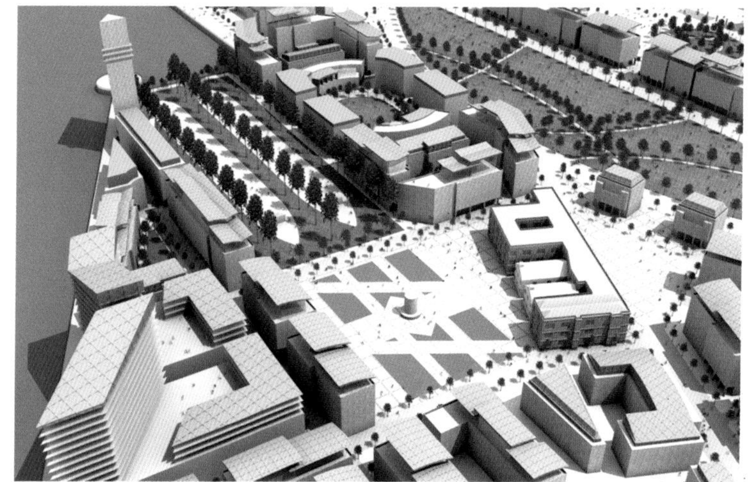

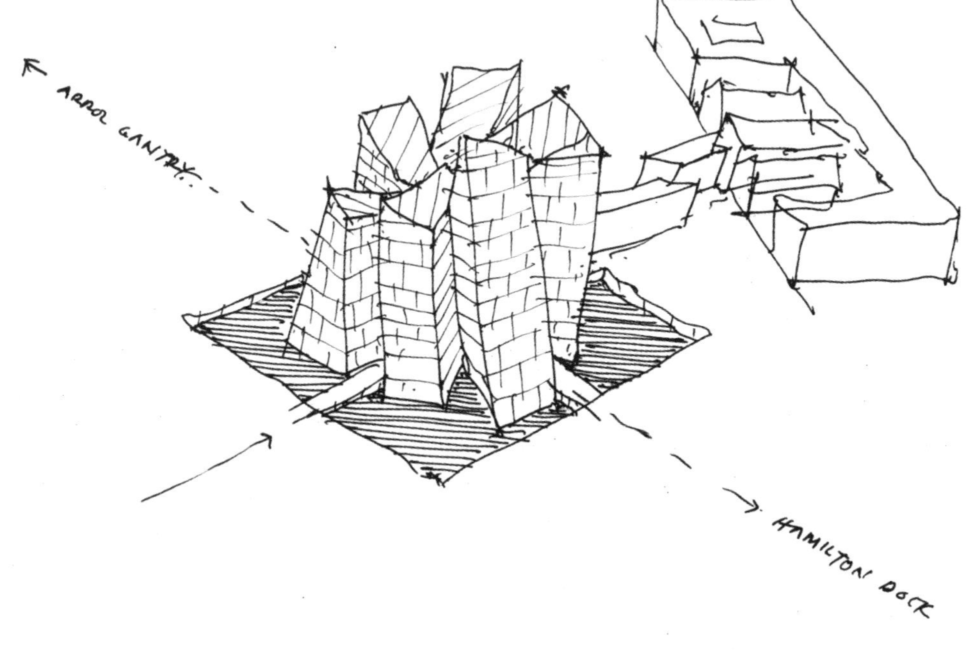

Light and dark

Encouraged by the warm reception at the Vision Plan launch, the design team were asked to press ahead. Sketch models in card and plastic became the preferred medium for exploring the crystalline forms, as this allowed the complexity of the irregular volumes to be appreciated. Later incarnations began to resemble less the quartz-like clusters and more the eroded surfaces of the floating pack ice that played such a fateful part in *Titanic*'s maiden voyage. CivicArts made an important observation early in the design process – they recognised the polarised character of the attraction they were trying to create. The exhibition spaces needed to be controlled environments, black boxes where the layers of artefacts, images, films and sounds could be carefully composed along a prescribed path. By contrast, the public spaces needed to be light and inviting, in order to encourage social interaction and free circulation with the surrounding plaza. The contrast between these two opposites provided the springboard for the early studies. These designs sought to collide two objects with these disparate properties in deliberate echo of how ship and iceberg had impacted upon each other. Here, the hard black boxes became the steel hull, embedded within the fragmented mass of ice. Shaped by great forces, the forms were jagged and dynamic. Though some designers might have shied away from ice because of its tragic connotations, the team felt it should be directly embraced. After all, if it were not for the iceberg, *Titanic*'s story would have been completely different.

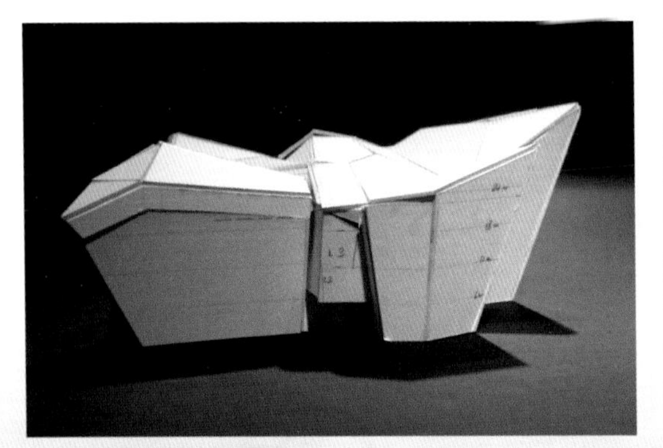

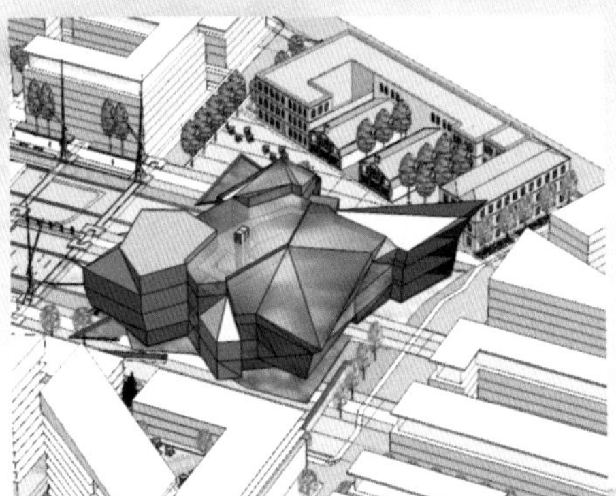

The earliest computer renderings of the large 'irregular iceberg' show it engulfing the water garden's pools in a long diagonal running north to south. The main body of the composition was glazed, with the more opaque fragments being envisaged as exhibition spaces.

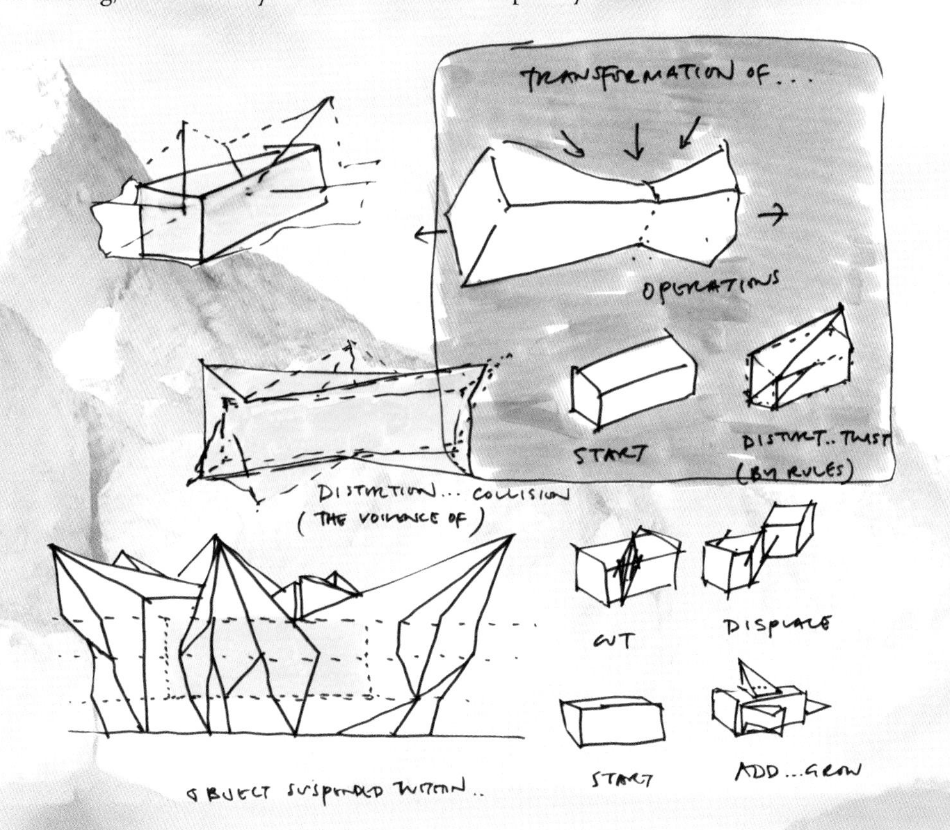

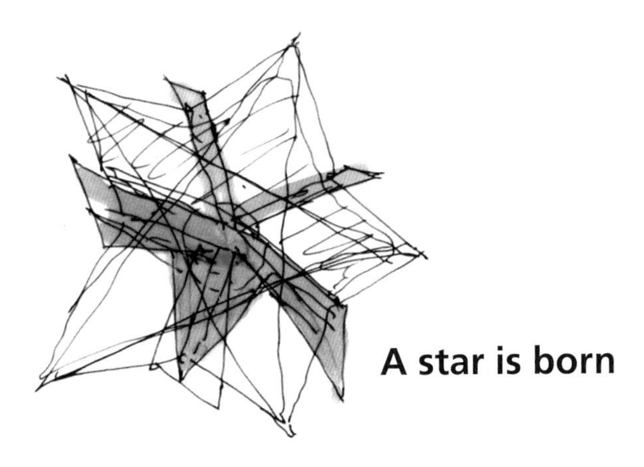

A star is born

Though sculptural and dynamic in three dimensions, the plans for the various irregular ice and crystalline forms did not translate easily into workable floor plates, wasting space and failing to align with the sightlines on the masterplan that the architects wished to preserve. Applying the logo of *Titanic*'s owners, the White Star Line, offered a means of taming this mass of fractured lines, whilst still promising an exciting sculptural form. A five-pointed star was laid in the midst of the water gardens and rotated to explore how those points might be aligned to other structures on the site. Diagonal walkways across the reflection pools had been generated by the sightlines from the drawing offices and old headquarters building intersecting with the dramatic views down the slipways to the Victoria Channel and beyond. To make the most of these important heritage vistas, the star's points were separated by glazed elements that divided them into 'black boxes', united by a central glazed atrium.

It was CivicArts's involvement as both concept architects and masterplanners that allowed them to take this holistic approach to the design process. The Signature Project was always viewed as the cultural hub for the new Titanic Quarter, rather than an abstract object dropped onto the site. Anticipating future developments around it, the team were effectively cutting the jewel to fit the setting.

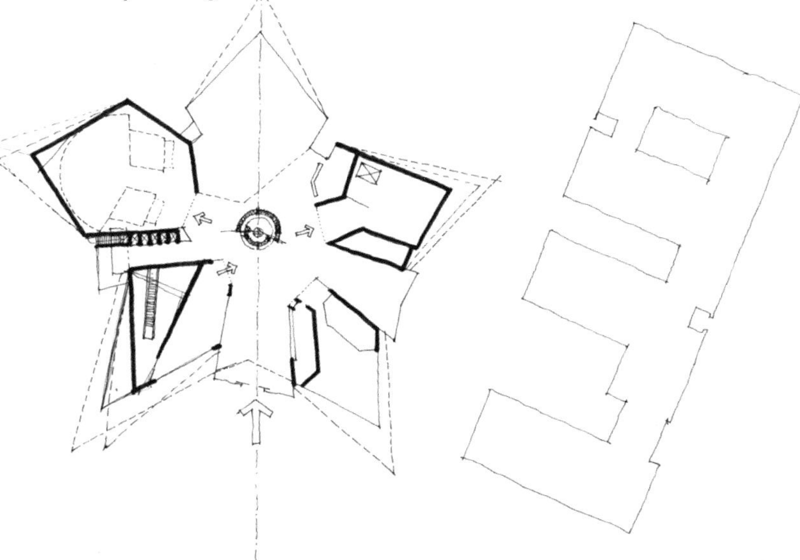

Crystals and compass roses

The wish to maximise the available viewing platforms gazing down the slipways led the team to experiment with the idea of completely glazing onc the star's five points, then enlarging it to dominate the cluster. The substantial footprint of the earlier models had caused concern, as they reduced the circulation spaces between the building and the historic drawing offices in an area envisaged as a busy public square. As the ground-floor plan contracted accordingly, the star's points started to splay out to maintain the same internal volume, and so the canted facades became ever more exaggerated. The sketch models became narrower and sharper, resembling the feathery knife-like flakes of frost that can form along ships' wires and cable stays.

The Signature Project's design was progressing in tandem with the masterplan and it became clear that the five-pointed form could not be made to correspond to the anticipated sightlines and circulation patterns of the surrounding developments. The decision was taken to shrink the glazed fifth point until it was almost absorbed into the cruciform atrium dividing the four opaque exhibition volumes. The result was increasingly reminiscent of the elaborate compass roses drawn on historic maps of Belfast, with the eight points loosely orientated to the cardinal directions. The White Star logo had served to rationalise the building's internal layout, but now its overt symbolism was beginning to be replaced by an equally appropriate metaphor – that of maritime navigation.

Standing between the hulls

Though no longer defining the overall form of the Signature Project, the Arrol Gantry still had a role to play in its evolution. The proportions of the tall, narrow glass fingers dividing the four jagged quadrants led the team to draw comparisons with the man-made canyon that had formed between the hulls of *Titanic* and *Olympic* as they rose side by side on the slipways. Could there be some way of recreating the intense atmosphere of this tall void, where gangs of riveters worked back to back on opposing hulls, filling it with the din of hammers as thick steel plates sailed past along the gantry's frames? The 'Giant Atrium' concept was born.

With an evocative family of external forms established, the shape of the Signature Project could be refined according to its content. Event Communications and CHL Consulting identified three major elements they perceived as desirable for the attraction to achieve true destination status. Accommodating their specific space requirements began to distort the building's geometry. The first element was an independent banqueting hall and public restaurant to capture the corporate hospitality market and help generate crucial revenue. These needed large, column-free spaces and were placed high up in the building where greater spans could be achieved. The second was the main gallery in Event's concept exhibition design, featuring immense scale models of *Titanic* and *Olympic* under construction, which visitors could fly over in an aerial ride. Contained within a two-storey high gallery, these spanned two of the four quadrants, bridging one of the glass divisions. The third was an advanced 'Flying Theatre' that would act as an independent attraction, with audience seating rising on hydraulic arms that moved them in sync with the action on a cinema screen. This required nearly an entire quadrant, extending down into the basement to create an 18-metre tall auditorium. With the Giant Atrium providing the unifying circulation spaces, this concept scheme was emerging as the first viable proposition for Queen's Island's centrepiece.

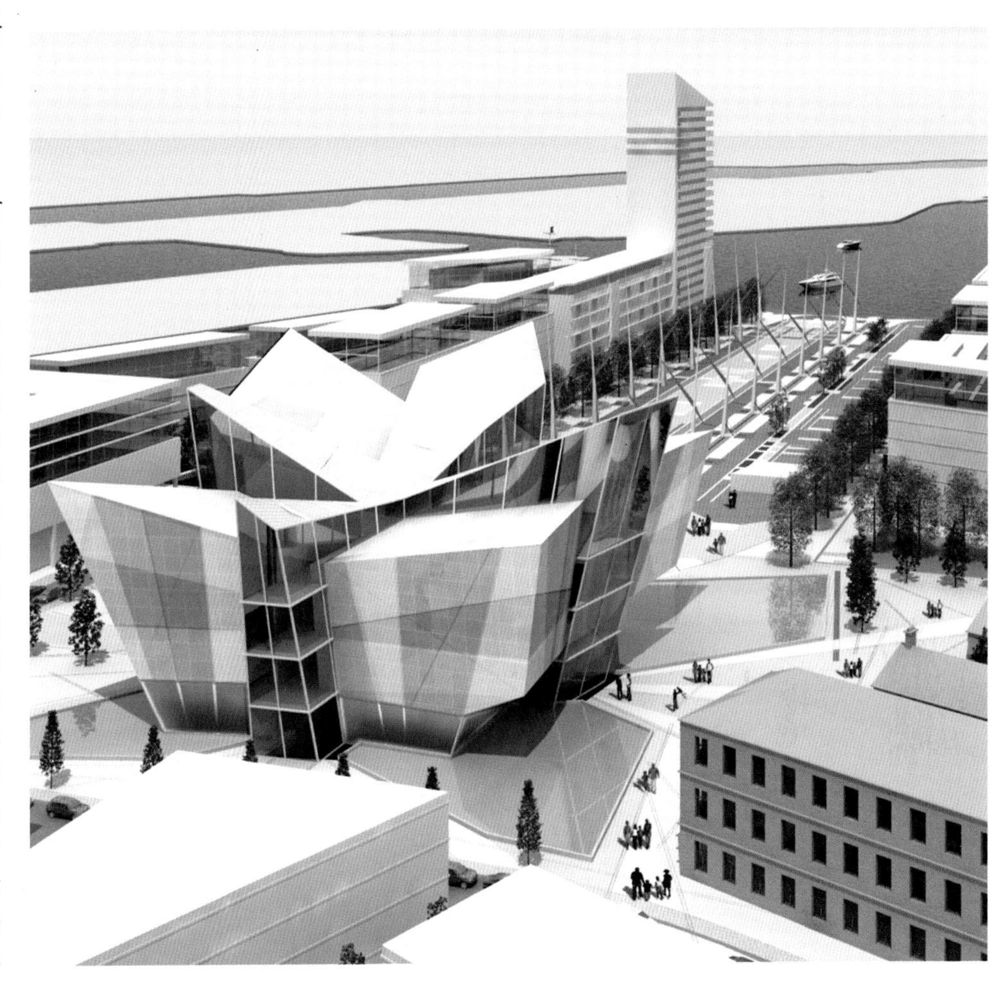

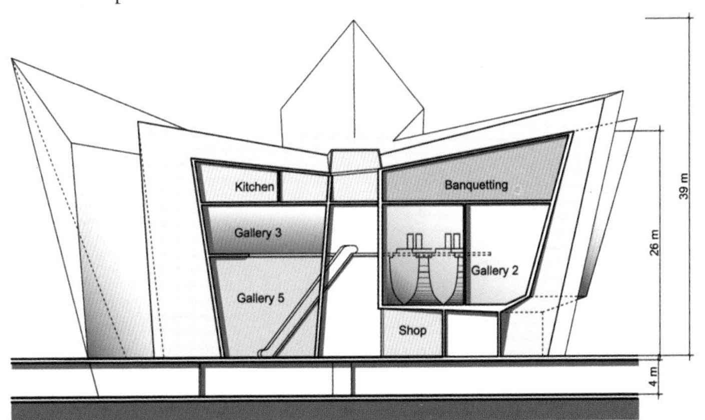

SECTION GALLERIES 2+3

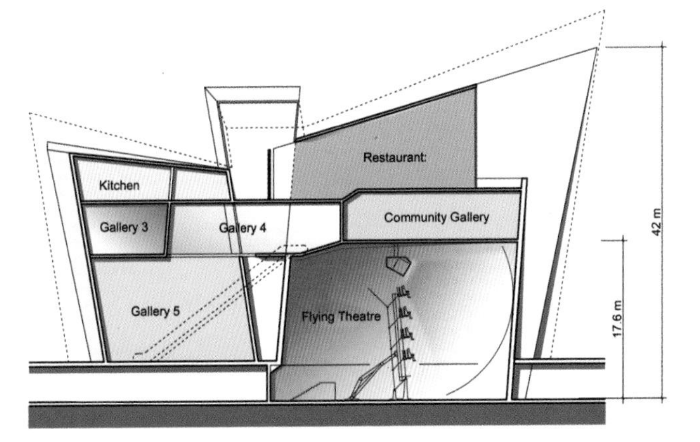

SECTION GALLERY 5 + CINEMA

These early cross sections show how the building's content requirements made it ever more asymmetrical. Dating from March 2006, these cross sections and the CGI render above hint at the complexity of layering distinctly different spaces within the irregular form. In order to be immersive, the galleries had to be linked sequentially to form a continuous narrative, which posed interesting challenges when designing internal circulation routes.

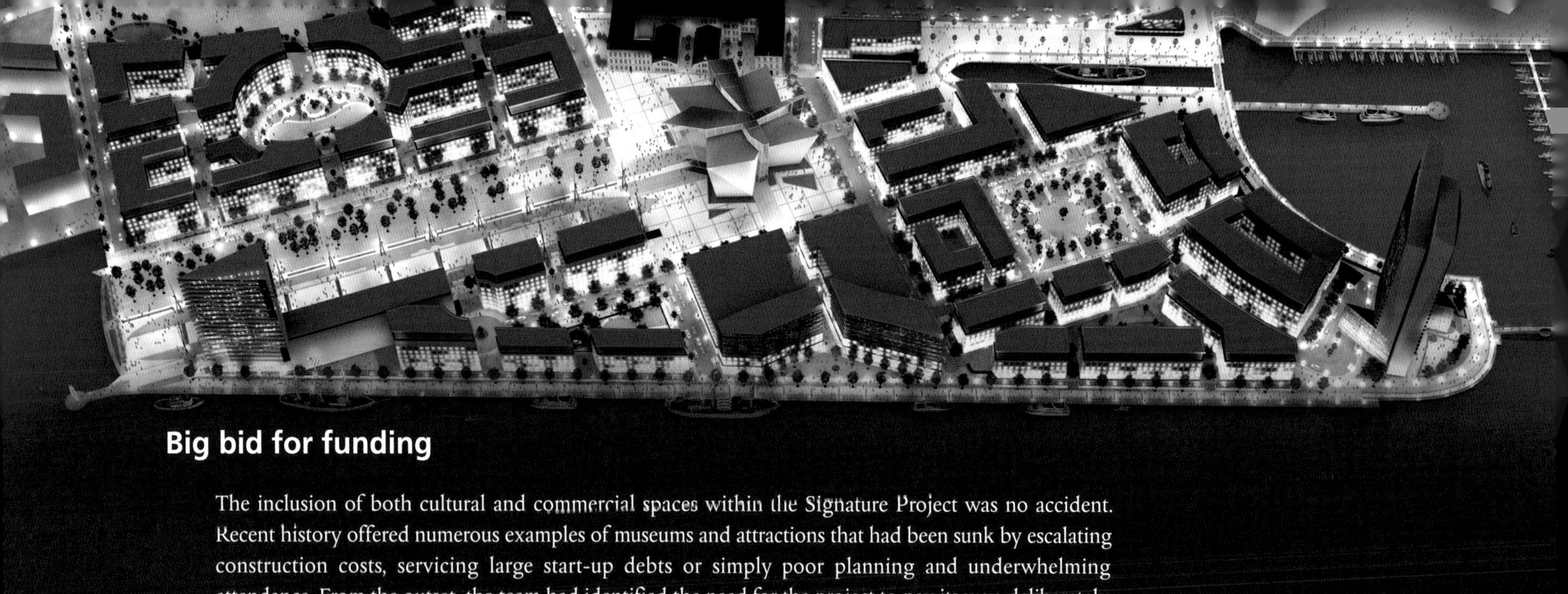

Big bid for funding

The inclusion of both cultural and commercial spaces within the Signature Project was no accident. Recent history offered numerous examples of museums and attractions that had been sunk by escalating construction costs, servicing large start-up debts or simply poor planning and underwhelming attendance. From the outset, the team had identified the need for the project to pay its way, deliberately including a mix of activities to make it capable of operating without further financial aid once launched. They envisaged that construction would be funded by an initial cash injection in the form of grants from various investors, after which the project would sustain itself through ticket sales and its strong appeal as a corporate/private venue.

One likely source of investment for this grand enterprise was the Big Lottery Fund. In January 2006 the Northern Ireland Tourist Board and CHL Consulting submitted the Signature Project for Stage 1 of the Living Landmarks Programme on behalf of the Titanic Alliance. Aiming to secure a £25 million grant towards construction, the team impressed the Landmark Review Committee that May with an eyecatching presentation, and in August it was announced that the scheme had been shortlisted along with two others in the Belfast area. Publicity aside, the most significant bonus to the process was the Big Lottery Fund's £250,000 grant to develop the plans further in preparation for Stage 2. Together with matched funding pooled by Titanic Quarter Ltd, NITB and the Belfast Harbour Commissioners, there were now the resources to pay for professional expertise. A team of 12 companies ranging from catering consultants to mechanical engineers could begin to develop the Titanic Signature Project in greater detail.

The Signature Project's hulls readily lent themselves to the design of graphic logos that dotted the Big Lottery Fund submission material. The potential to project imagery onto the large, flat surfaces of the building's jutting quadrants was also recognised at a very early stage. This concept was carried through to reality with spectacular light shows during the *Titanic* centenary commemorations.

From shards to ships

Taken in 1898, this image of the ships *Afric*, *Oceanic* and *Medic* under construction shows Harland & Wolff's North Yard prior to its 1906 reconfiguration to prepare for the Arrol Gantry and *Titanic*.

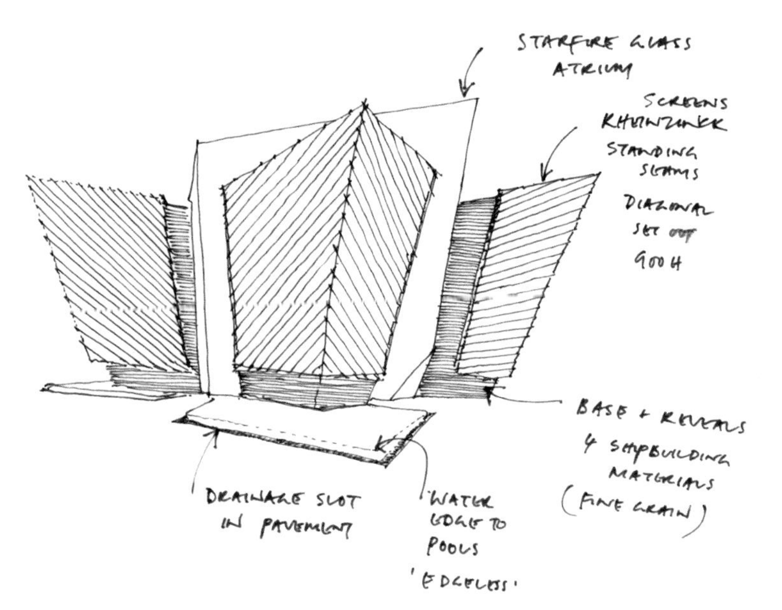

One of the most significant outcomes of the year-long design development for the Stage 2 bid was to be the evolution of the Signature Project's outward appearance. The sloping facades had been a consistent element of the design since the early crystalline forms, with the stacking of ever-larger floor plates naturally leading to an outwardly stepped composition, smoothed into pointed shards by the external cladding. With the help of the team's engineers and technical consultants, CivicArts began a process of rationalising the form in an effort to reduce the facade's surface area and thereby make significant cost savings. The shapes gradually became cleaner and the building more compact. The dramatic sharp points retracted as the quadrants swelled to accommodate new internal elements. Slowly the forms began to resemble not shards, but ships. The effect became ever more exaggerated until the overall plan resembled four prows, united by a single 'diamond crystal' in which the column-free banqueting hall found a natural home. The composition created pleasing parallels with the historic images of ships under construction, their diverging prows clothed in cradles of wooden scaffolding. Evocatively described as 'cribbage' by Eric Kuhne, these timber lattices were later reimagined as wooden louvres inside the atrium.

The four distinct hulls presented new opportunities for extending a material narrative to the exterior. At one stage the concept of representing the 'four ages of shipbuilding' was considered, with the hulls being sequentially faced in timber, wrought iron, steel and aluminium to represent the advances in shipbuilding science. Though ultimately plated almost entirely in anodised aluminium, two of the steel-framed hulls retain this timber planking down their narrow return faces.

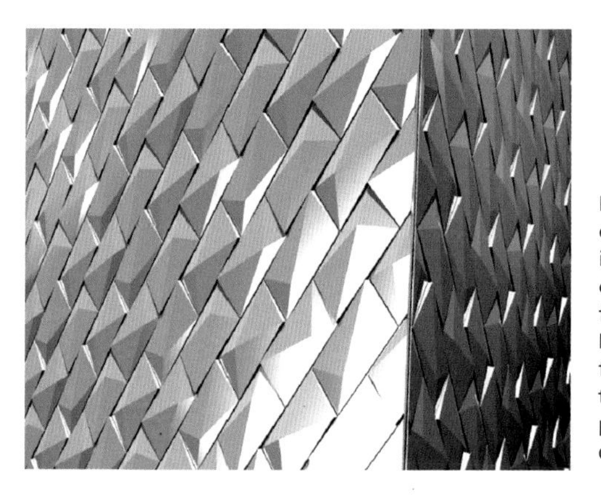

From polished quartz crystals to fragmenting ice sheets, the selection of faceted, folded forms for the Signature Project's outer skin forged multiple links to the natural and historic precedents driving the design process.

'The most powerful way that an engineer can contribute to the work of architects is by exploring the nature of the materials and using that knowledge to produce a special quality.'

Peter Rice (1935–92), Founder, RFR Group

Plating the bows

With naval architecture now dominating the design, the team now considered how these four stately bows might be plated. Metal would clearly be a practical and appropriate choice; several of the sketch models had already been clothed in sheets of smooth or perforated steel. Interlocking strips of zinc would be another option, but somehow the hard diagonal standing seams of the early sketches were too perfunctory, too factory-like for such a landmark building, and failed to flatter its bulk. Seeking a more poetic solution, CivicArts collaborated with their engineering consultants, RFR Group, and revisited the collection of ice and crystal imagery that had set the project on its present course.

RFR came back with an intriguing proposal. Why not sheath the building in a skin of three-dimensional panels made from sheets of folded aluminium, creating a faceted facade that caught the light? The concept caught the imagination of both teams. Here was something that might add a special quality to the prestigious Signature Project. The two firms spent weeks working on numerous permutations, from simple diagonal folds to four-facet crystals, arranging them in courses along the sloping bows. Having completed its budgeted scope of work, RFR signed off from the Signature Project in April 2007, leaving the design development and visualisation of the panelled facade to CivicArts. Though its time on the project was relatively brief, RFR had made an important contribution to what would ultimately become Titanic Belfast's signature style.

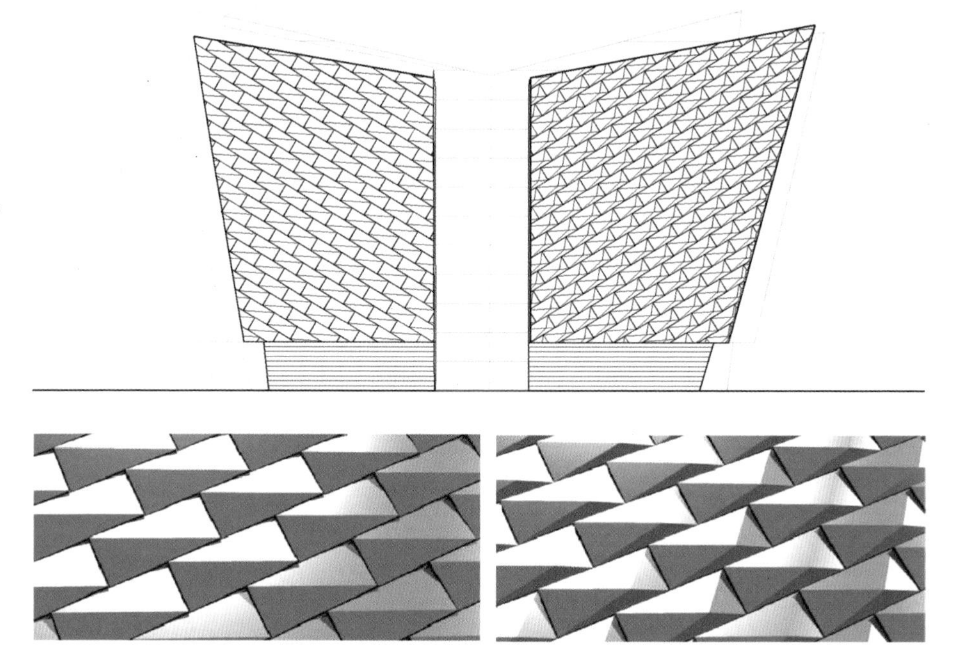

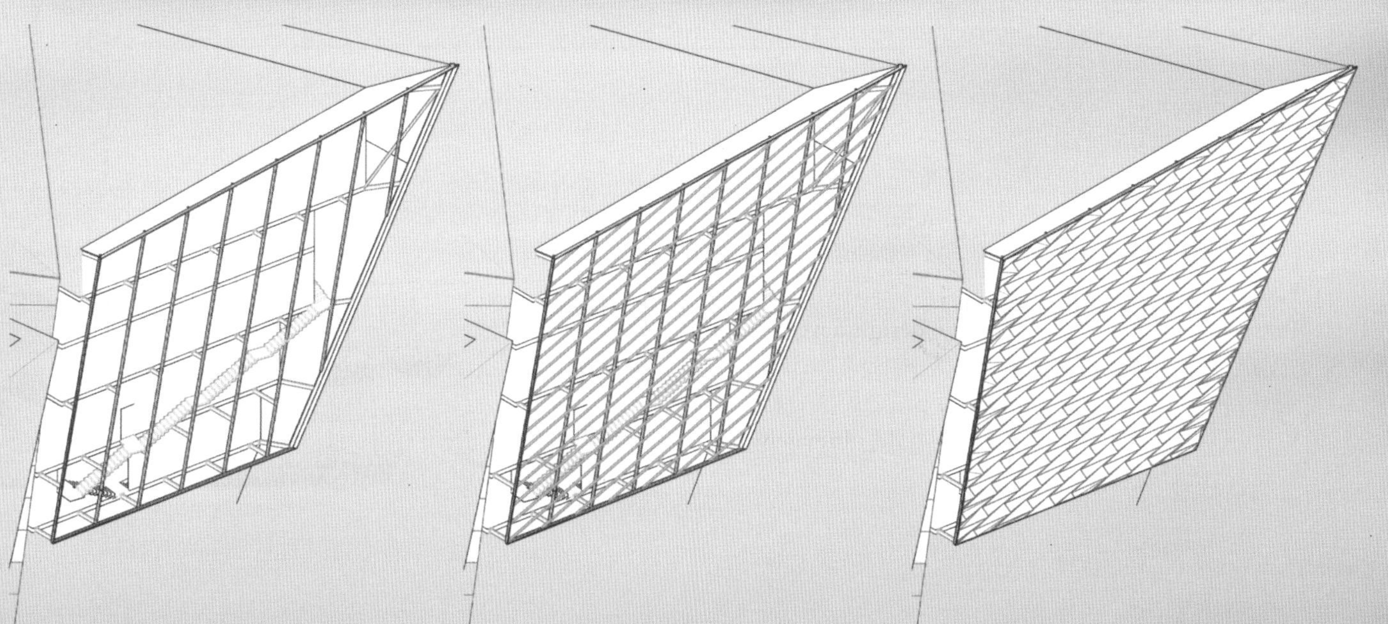

RFR devised an assembly sequence by which this sculptural rain screen could be realised. A projecting steelwork frame was anchored to the floor plates to create the necessary vertical profile, after which a secondary layer of diagonal rails would be attached. The lines of aluminium panels would be hung on these rails. Breaking the facade down into lightweight component form served to strengthen the visual parallels with the heavy engineering of the shipyards.

Bad news from Big Lottery

With its hulls clad in gleaming aluminium panels, the Titanic Signature Project looked to be in great shape for the next stage of the Living Landmarks process. CHL Consulting and NITB duly filed the Stage 2 application in time for the 31st May 2007 deadline, and the Signature Project team prepared for the crucial presentation to be held that July. The bid was put forward in the name of Titanic Foundation Ltd – a charitable trust who were to be the future owners and operators of the building and would promote Belfast's *Titanic*, maritime and industrial heritage to a world audience.

Titanic House is part of the former Harland & Wolff headquarters building and is home to the offices of Titanic Quarter Ltd. From the stage-two presentation, the TSP Team filled the building's reception area with an impressive display of architectural models, posters and drawings, backed by evocative displays of period costumes and Edwardian ephemera. Lights shining through the model's Perspex base helped throw the tiny scale panels into high relief, illustrating the proposed building's graphic nocturnal potential.

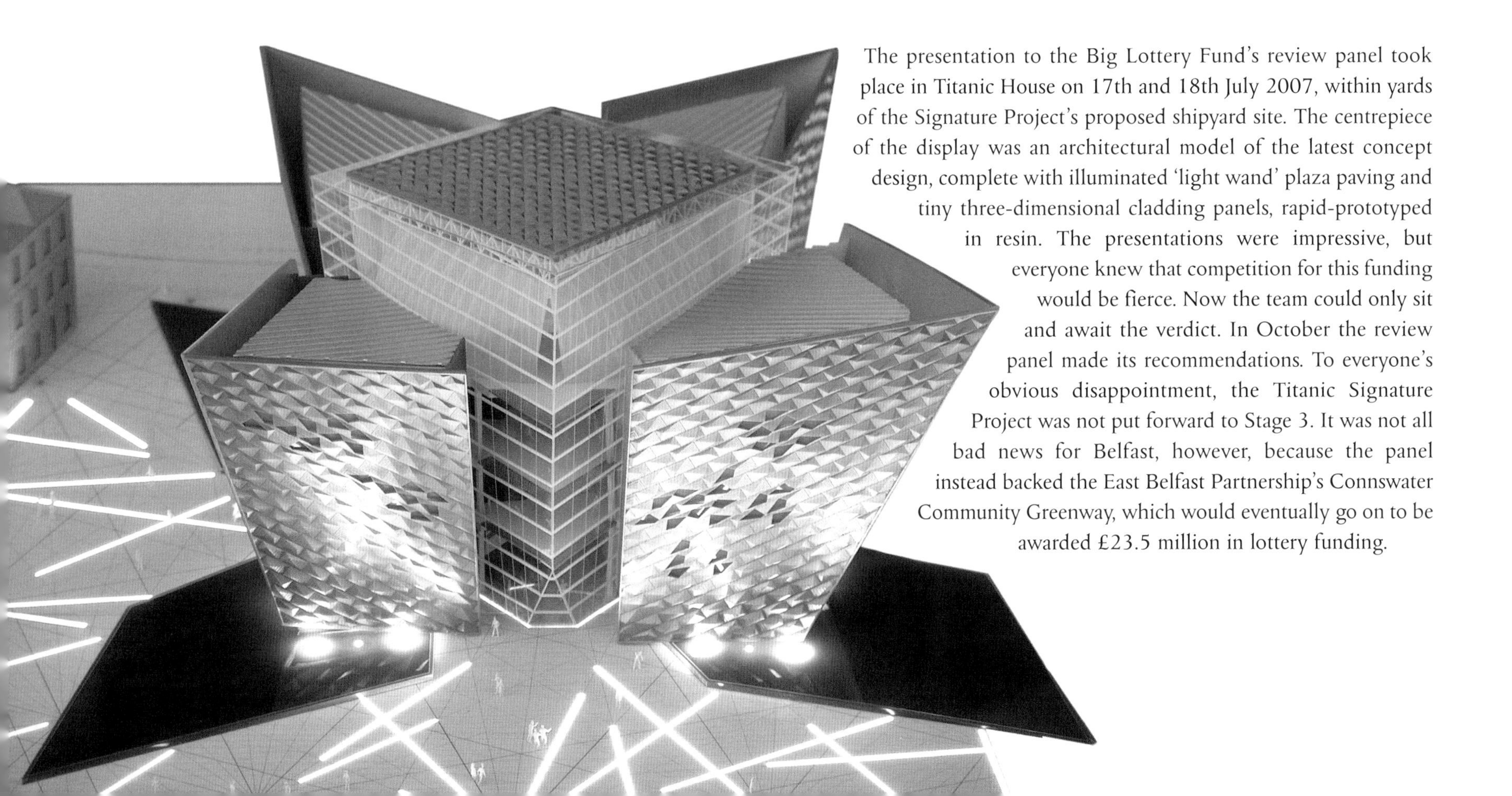

The presentation to the Big Lottery Fund's review panel took place in Titanic House on 17th and 18th July 2007, within yards of the Signature Project's proposed shipyard site. The centrepiece of the display was an architectural model of the latest concept design, complete with illuminated 'light wand' plaza paving and tiny three-dimensional cladding panels, rapid-prototyped in resin. The presentations were impressive, but everyone knew that competition for this funding would be fierce. Now the team could only sit and await the verdict. In October the review panel made its recommendations. To everyone's obvious disappointment, the Titanic Signature Project was not put forward to Stage 3. It was not all bad news for Belfast, however, because the panel instead backed the East Belfast Partnership's Connswater Community Greenway, which would eventually go on to be awarded £23.5 million in lottery funding.

Life after the Lottery

Though understandably a setback, the failure of the Big Lottery Fund bid was not the end of the line. The momentum and enthusiasm built up over the lottery proposal process had convinced many influential bodies that this might be too good an opportunity for the city to miss. Even without Big Lottery funding, there was still life in this potential landmark. The detailed design and operating plans required for the lottery grant application had advanced the project to the point that it was ready to break ground. Titanic Quarter's Deputy Chairman, Conal Harvey, and Chief Executive, Mike Smith, now began a concerted effort to build support for the scheme. Offering the tantalising prospect of an international destination on Belfast's doorstep, they led negotiations with funding partners and stakeholders to find a way to a financial solution.

The first task was to review the scheme and refine the projected construction costs, which the Northern Ireland Audit Office would later record as £76.9 million, excluding the value of the land and pre-construction design development. In order to meet the project's growing needs, contributions from the various stakeholders had to increase. The Department of Enterprise, Trade and Investment (DETI) and NITB jointly promised up to £43 million. Titanic Quarter Ltd offered £16.35 million, and the Belfast Harbour Commissioners £13.6 million. Belfast City Council now joined this trio, with a provisional offer of £10 million. With such large sums at stake, many safeguards and guarantees had to be in place and it was obtaining these various assurances that stretched the process into weeks, then months. Many of the contributions were conditional upon every other party remaining at the table; it was a case of all or nothing. The power of the Signature Project can be measured by the fact that it created such a remarkable alignment of interests between public and private bodies that this complex funding package came to fruition.

The granting of outline planning approval for the Titanic Quarter phase-two masterplan on 28th June 2008 effectively established the principle of building the Signature Project at the head of the slipways. Five months later, on 27th November, the Northern Ireland Executive committed the public funds of DETI and NITB to the project. However, this commitment was being made against the background of a deepening global financial crisis triggered by the dramatic collapse of Lehman Brothers that September. The Irish banking crisis that followed further complicated matters, with more administrative hurdles being created as those underwriting loans became increasingly averse to taking risks. Again, the need for guarantees and issues of procurement processes had to be addressed and, though the Signature Project continued to plough on through these troubled financial waters, time was rapidly running out. Recognising that completing the project in time for *Titanic*'s centenary commemoration was crucial to its success, Pat Doherty made a bold decision. Committing his own money, he ordered Harcourt Construction (NI) to begin preparatory work, clearing the site and excavating the underground car park long before the government funding had been approved. His decision undoubtedly saved the project. By the time the Executive finally confirmed its contribution of £36.95 million on 1st October 2009, the diggers had already been at work for six months, keeping the future Titanic Belfast on track.

'The vision and commitment of Pat Doherty and Conal Harvey from Titanic Quarter ensured that this building was started, at risk and ahead of funding approval. Had this not happened, we might still be waiting for the official launch.'

Paul Crowe, Managing Director, Todd Architects

Todd's *Titanic* team of Daragh Coleman, Colin Gibson, Kari Simpson, Paul Crowe, Matthew Davis and Angus Waddington worked closely with CivicArts to make the Signature Project's plans watertight.

A new team comes on board

While the long process of securing funding rumbled on behind the scenes, time had not stood still for the TSP Team. Having convinced many influential bodies to throw their weight behind the scheme, CivicArts' detailed concept design now had to be taken to the next stage of development, with the production of cost-able construction drawings that would fit the likely budget. This task would require additional skills and experience and a solid grounding in the myriad building-code standards that must be met when applying for planning consent.

The team found their ideal collaborators in Todd Architects, who had been involved in the development of Titanic Quarter since its inception. Working with Harcourt Construction (NI), Todd were already engaged as architects for the new Public Record Office of Northern Ireland, as well as Belfast Metropolitan College's new city-centre campus – both vital components of the regeneration of Queen's Island. With offices in Dublin and Belfast, Todd could provide both the local knowledge and the depth of technical expertise the Signature Project would require. First contacted in April 2008, Todd Architects were officially appointed as lead consultants that August and quickly formed a very close working relationship with CivicArts. Their major role was to finalise the complete scheme design and undertake detailed design-development work. Together with a host of technical specialists including consultant engineers RPS and AECOM and the contractor's project managers, Sweett Group, the new team began to edge the Signature Project towards construction.

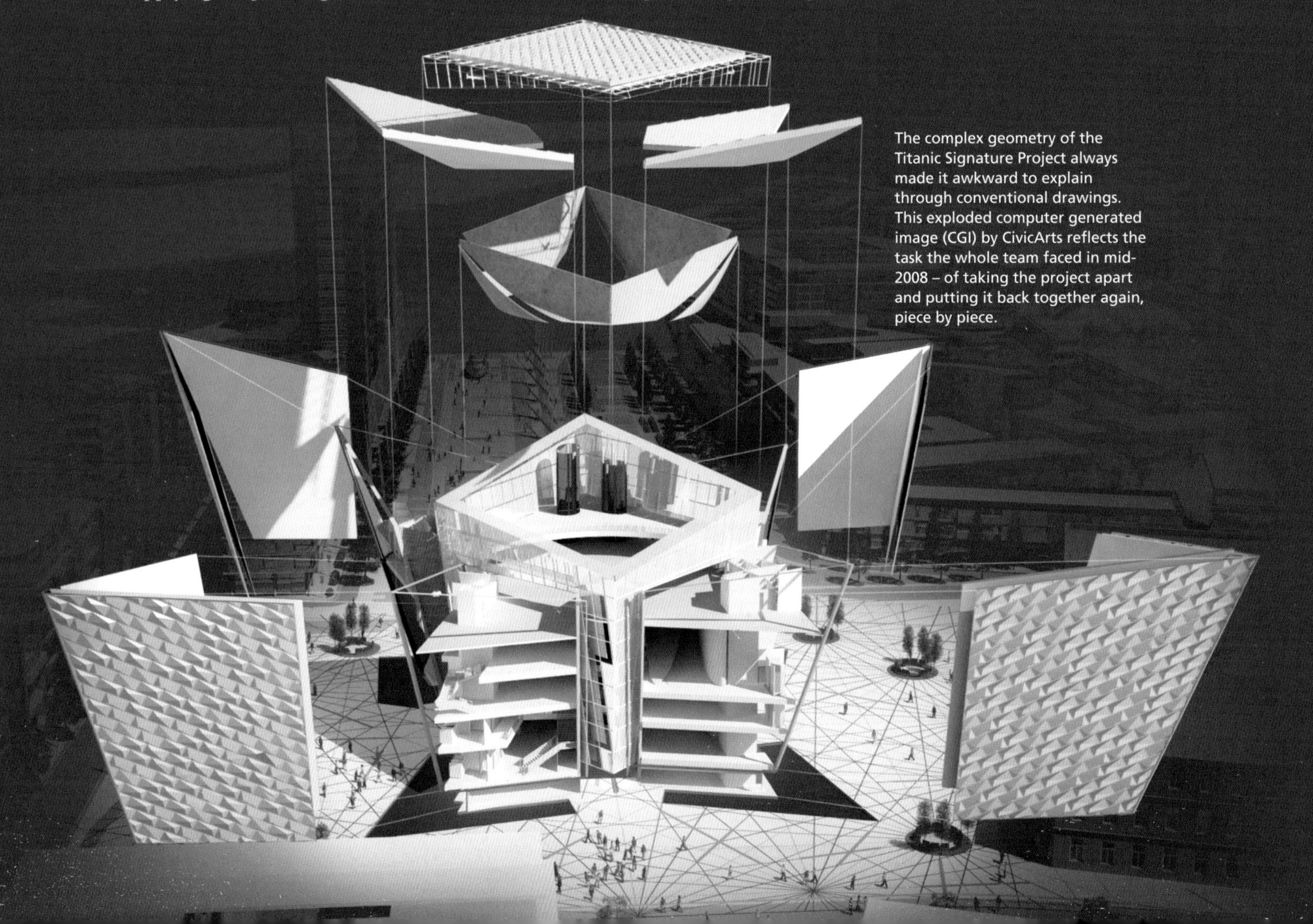

The complex geometry of the Titanic Signature Project always made it awkward to explain through conventional drawings. This exploded computer generated image (CGI) by CivicArts reflects the task the whole team faced in mid-2008 – of taking the project apart and putting it back together again, piece by piece.

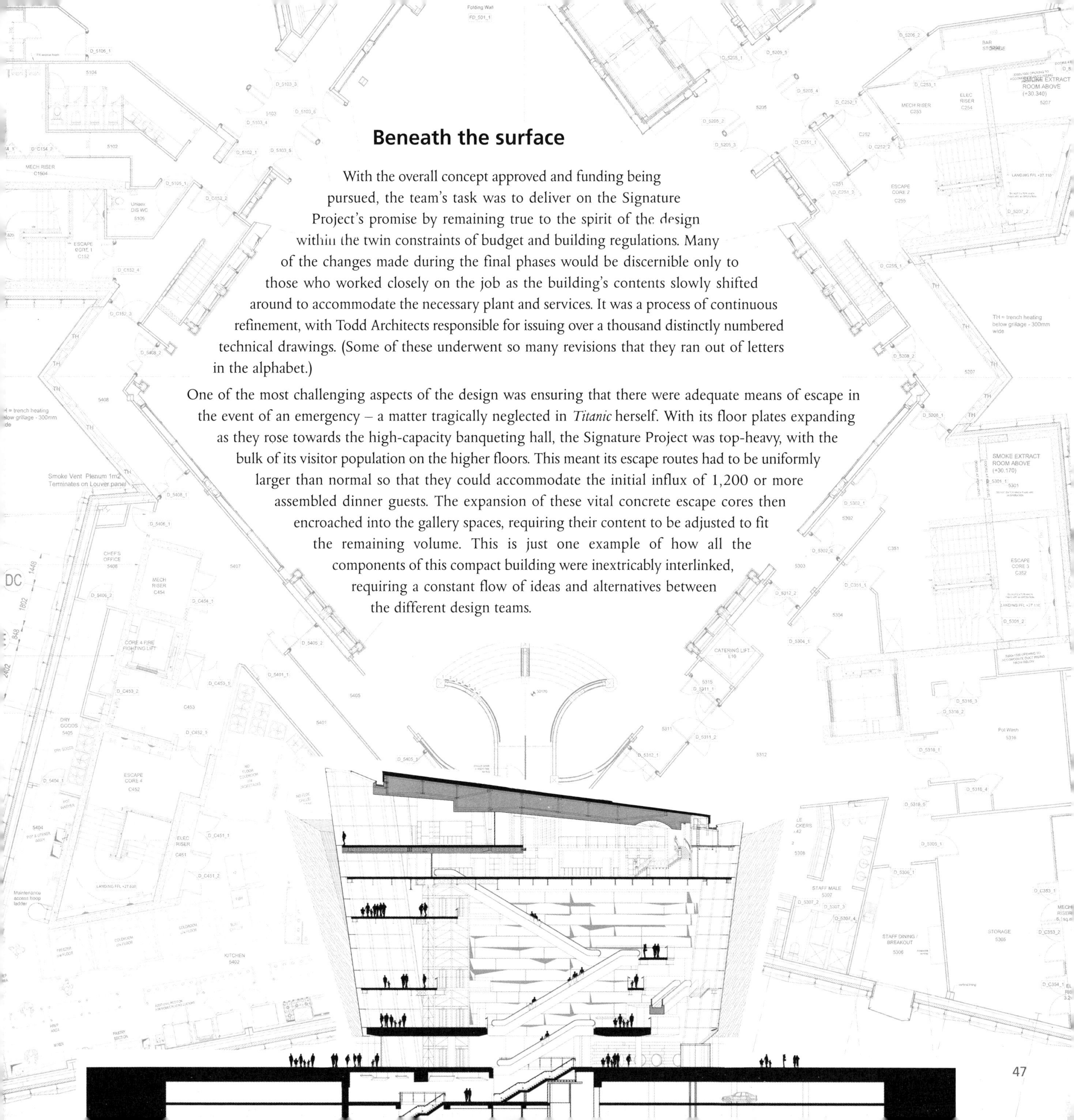

Beneath the surface

With the overall concept approved and funding being pursued, the team's task was to deliver on the Signature Project's promise by remaining true to the spirit of the design within the twin constraints of budget and building regulations. Many of the changes made during the final phases would be discernible only to those who worked closely on the job as the building's contents slowly shifted around to accommodate the necessary plant and services. It was a process of continuous refinement, with Todd Architects responsible for issuing over a thousand distinctly numbered technical drawings. (Some of these underwent so many revisions that they ran out of letters in the alphabet.)

One of the most challenging aspects of the design was ensuring that there were adequate means of escape in the event of an emergency – a matter tragically neglected in *Titanic* herself. With its floor plates expanding as they rose towards the high-capacity banqueting hall, the Signature Project was top-heavy, with the bulk of its visitor population on the higher floors. This meant its escape routes had to be uniformly larger than normal so that they could accommodate the initial influx of 1,200 or more assembled dinner guests. The expansion of these vital concrete escape cores then encroached into the gallery spaces, requiring their content to be adjusted to fit the remaining volume. This is just one example of how all the components of this compact building were inextricably interlinked, requiring a constant flow of ideas and alternatives between the different design teams.

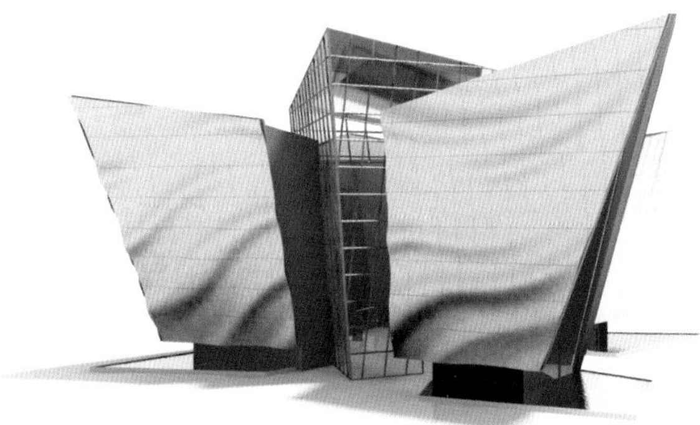

Folds and facets

The long development of the distinctive aluminium cladding was a collaborative effort between CivicArts and Todd Architects, combining technical input from contractors and engineers. The challenge was to develop a panel that would integrate with the irregular geometry of the four hulls and still be compatible with the existing railing systems then available. Cost had to be considered, but such a prominent landmark building deserved a bespoke solution.

The rectangular and trapezoidal panels were not the only avenues explored during the cladding's long gestation. One alternative concept was the 'wave facade', where the sectioned metal skin was made to undulate like magnified ripples on a pool of water. As the proportions of the original cladding panels evolved, the way they were be orientated on each facade was also debated. One permutation saw the panels laid vertically, with their long sides parallel to the leading edge of each hull, but this arrangement changed the character of the form quite dramatically.

The first panels were compact 2:1 ratio rectangles but these were felt to be too small and brick-like. Enlarging and elongating them to reduce the number of joints lent a dynamic aspect to the structure, emphasising the upward sweep of its canted hulls. Though echoing the steel stakes of *Titanic*'s bows, it was the maximum dimensions of the coiled raw material and processing machinery that drove the final panel proportions. But to what element of the four hulls should these panels be aligned, given that all eight facades had different angles to their tops and leading edges? The crucial decision was to switch from rectangular to trapezoidal panels, then experiment with aligning them to either one or both edges to find a natural fit. The final solution saw the panels laid at a constant 30-degree angle across every facade, with the angle of their short sides adjusted to correspond to the leading edge of the relevant hull. As the angle of each hull's leading edge was different, this made the panels unique to each facade. Randomly arranging the new trapezoid panels by raising or lowering their corners by 300 millimetres made the cut and folded facets catch the light. The team had found the ideal combination of form, folds and functionality.

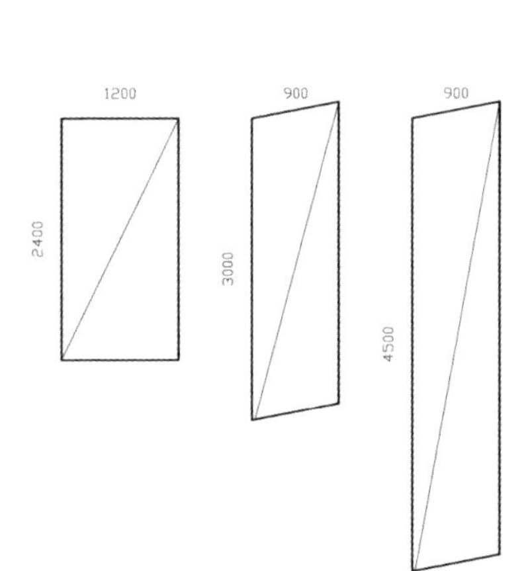

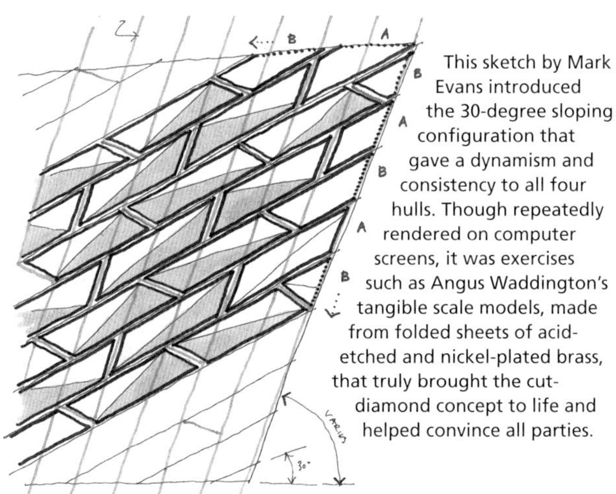

This sketch by Mark Evans introduced the 30-degree sloping configuration that gave a dynamism and consistency to all four hulls. Though repeatedly rendered on computer screens, it was exercises such as Angus Waddington's tangible scale models, made from folded sheets of acid-etched and nickel-plated brass, that truly brought the cut-diamond concept to life and helped convince all parties.

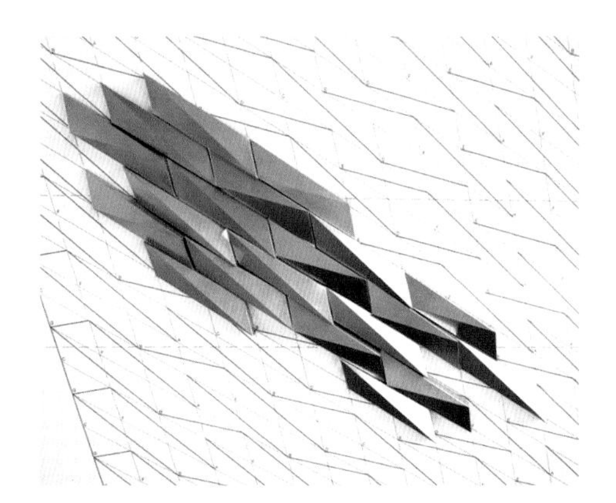

The final panel design produced a richly textured surface that offered up a mass of metaphors, from breaking waves and eroded pack ice to cut diamonds and crystal shards. Imbuing the bows with a sense of movement, it created an abstract sea of reflected light.

Delicate pieces of architectural origami, Angus Waddington's paper studies showed how exciting three-dimensional forms could be fabricated from a single sheet of aluminium. Using this box-net construction required minimal welding, with the seams discreetly hidden around the edges. Simply varying the shape of those folded edges either raised or lowered the panel corners, giving much greater depth and surface variation. The folds also provided the structural rigidity to make the elongated panels viable.

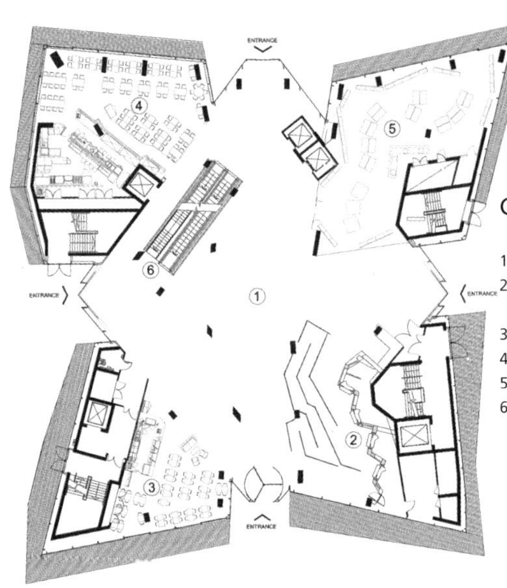

Ground floor

1 Welcome hall/atrium
2 Ticket desk & tourist information
3 Café
4 Bistro restaurant
5 Gift shop
6 Escalators to galleries & from basement

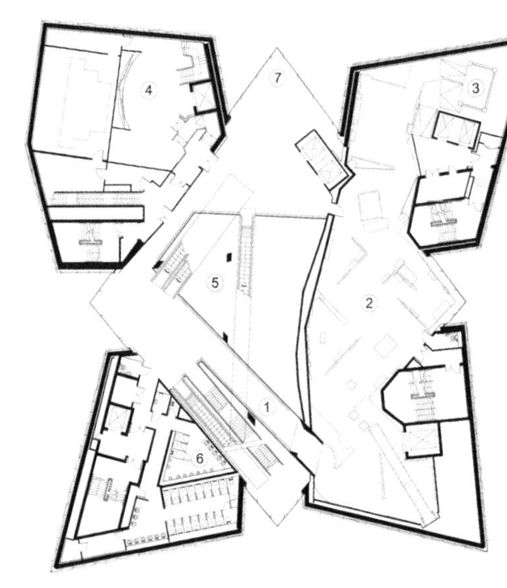

First floor

1 Entrance to galleries
2 Gallery – Boomtown Belfast
3 Arrol Gantry
4 Ocean Exploration Centre
5 Void & escalators
6 WCs
7 Slipway viewing area

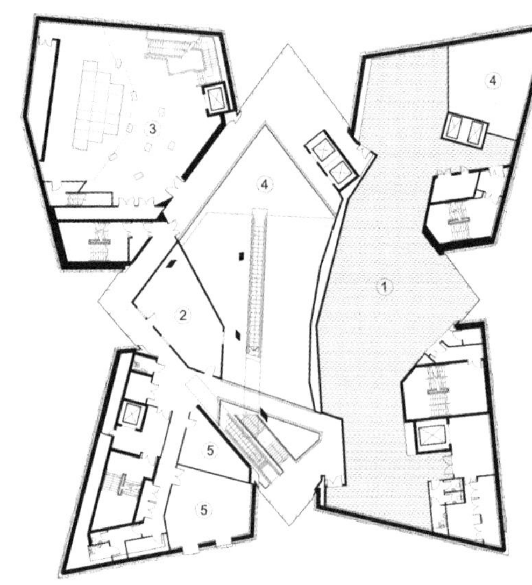

Second floor

1 Andrews Gallery (temporary exhibition)
2 Education suite
3 Gallery – Rediscovering the Wreck
4 Void
5 Offices

Third floor

1 Dark Ride – gallery floor & set pieces
2 Gallery – The Aftermath & Inquiries
3 Gallery – Myths & Legends
4 Gallery – Immersive theatre
5 Offices
6 Void

Fourth floor

1 Arrol Gantry walkway
2 Gallery – Dark Ride
3 Gallery – The Launch
4 Gallery – The Fit-Out
5 Gallery – Maiden Voyage
6 Gallery – The Sinking
7 Void

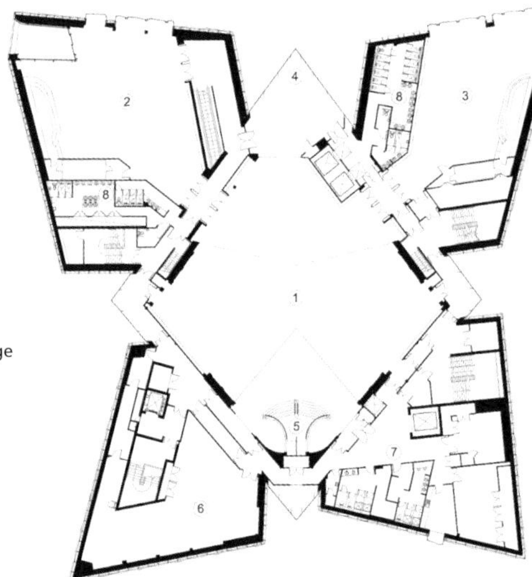

Fifth floor

1 Banquet hall dining – The Bridge
2 Banquet hall pre-function – The *Olympic* Suite
3 Banquet hall pre-function – The *Britannic* Suite
4 Slipway viewing area & meet & greet
5 Grand Staircase
6 Kitchen
7 Staff facilities
8 WCs

The busy density of these floor plans conveys how every corner of this compact building was pressed into service, in spite of the unconventional geometry. The combination of acute angles and canted walls created irregular and exciting interiors that Event's galleries were able to exploit to the full. Aside from the cathedral-like atrium, the largest single volume was reserved for the snaking aerial shipyard ride, whose cars rise and fall within a void spanning the third and fourth floors.

An icon for Queen's Island

After months and years of patient work, the Titanic Signature Project had at last evolved into its final form. Pat Doherty had asked for an icon: a beacon for Belfast and a triumphant centrepiece for Titanic Quarter. Few who saw Eric Kuhne's casual freehand crystal sketches in the autumn of 2005 could have imagined the distance this idea would travel in the search for global-landmark status. From white stars and icebergs to crystals and compass roses, each successive concept phase had left its mark in plan or detail. All these emblems lent their collected meanings to tell a richer narrative.

With echoes of crystal palaces, Edwardian liners and Atlantic ice floes, the final form was a mass of multiple metaphors, left open to interpretation in the eye of the beholder. With the glowing lantern of the central atrium uniting the four gleaming aluminium hulls, the nocturnal vision of the building was as majestic as the stately ships that in part inspired it. It was now the task of Harcourt Construction (NI) to transform these potent virtual renders into iconic concrete reality.

Vision to reality

Time was the one thing money could not buy for Titanic Belfast. With the immovable centenary of the ship's maiden voyage just over the horizon, there was little margin for error. Everything would have to run according to plan if the opening was to be the red-letter day event that everyone desired. Pat Doherty's bold decision to begin the foundations before full funding was confirmed had already saved precious months. With the money in place in October 2009, the race to build the world's largest *Titanic*-themed attraction now began in earnest.

The full weight of Harcourt Construction (NI) was put to the task of realising Titanic Quarter's centrepiece. Together with Todd Architects, RPS Engineers, Sweett Group and many other consultants, specialists and contractors, they embarked upon a construction schedule whose pace was set by the ticking clock of history. With its irregular geometry and complex fit-out, Titanic Belfast would present many challenges. The speed and skill with which they were all overcome would fill a book in itself. The following pages can offer but a hint of the frenetic activity and enterprising engineering that now lie serenely hidden beneath the shimmering facades.

Belfast's harsh winter was no friend to the construction team, who laboured long in atrocious conditions to keep the build on schedule. The mat of steel reinforcement for the basement slab had to be freed from its layer of ice and snow before any concrete could be poured.

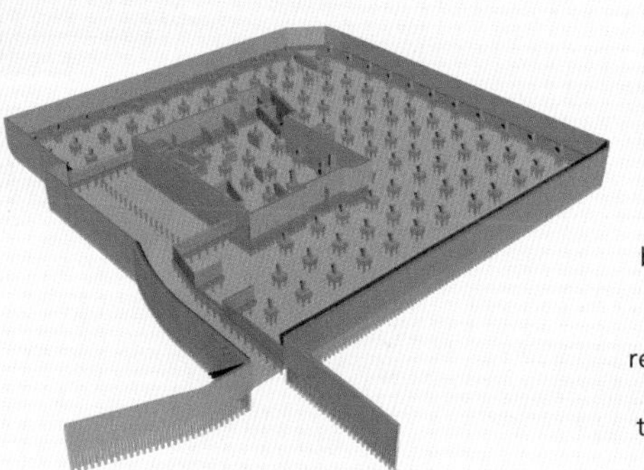

Protruding above the walls of concrete-filled secant piles, the funnel and superstructure of a passing ferry neatly illustrate how work had to be carried out well beneath the water table. The dense metre-thick cage of steel reinforcement bars would securely tie the slab to the exposed heads of the load-bearing piles.

Island excavations

From a historical perspective, Queen's Island was the perfect site for a *Titanic*-themed attraction, but the realities of its man-made composition posed unique challenges for the construction team. Known locally as 'sleech' or 'slob', this soft reclaimed land was permanently saturated with water thanks to its low-lying position beside the tidal River Lagan. In the process of building a sufficiently deep foundation to support Titanic Belfast and accommodate a 520-space car park beneath, the design team effectively had to create a watertight concrete hull that would be submerged beneath the water table. This hull had natural buoyancy, being subjected to an uplift force as the waterlogged soil tried to push it to the surface. Counter-intuitive though it may seem, the monolithic mass of Titanic Belfast would have to be weighed down with concrete ballast to prevent her from floating away.

The first task was to create a stable perimeter using secant piling, which was driven into the ground to form a retaining wall outlining an area over 100 metres square. With this in place, Harcourt Construction (NI) could then safely excavate to eight metres below ground level, removing some 145,000 tons of earth in the process. Into the floor of this vast pit were driven 1,025 load-bearing piles that would anchor Titanic Belfast in the boulder clay 30 metres down.

As the man in charge of the build, Construction Manager Noel Molloy chose to stay on site throughout the whole pour. He joined the team in the pit, directing the concrete as it was pumped into the vast areas of steel reinforcement to create the monolithic slab.

The big pour

There was an undeniable element of sci-fi drama to the big pour as the sun went down, and the synchronised dance of the pumping rigs continued under the glare of floodlights. Dwarfed by the arching rigs, teams of contractors in high-visibility jackets scurried about beneath the giant arms, vibrating and compacting the concrete in readiness for the next delivery.

The ballast for Titanic Belfast would be its massive basement slabs. The lowest of these was cast in five layers, reaching a thickness of 1.1 metres. With the 2,500 tons of steel reinforcement in place, the stage was set for the largest single concrete pour in Irish history. To ensure the smooth delivery of the 4,200 cubic metres of concrete required, the pour was carried out over a weekend in December 2009, reducing the risk of the 700 separate lorry-loads being delayed by traffic in Belfast city centre. Working continuously over a 24-hour period, the concrete was ferried to the site at a rate of one lorry every two minutes, by a team of fifty drivers working eight-hour shifts. Once onsite, the mix was distributed by eight massive pumping rigs with long hydraulic arms that could reach out into the middle of the slab. The slab was a composite, with the first 300-millimetre layer being composed of waterproof concrete, overlaid with ordinary concrete to achieve the necessary thickness. A dramatic moment in the build, this pour of biblical proportions recaptured some of the scale and ambition that this shipyard had once witnessed.

Setting the table

Though equivalent in height to a ten or eleven-storey building, the four hulls of Titanic Belfast succeed in floating above the plaza, mirrored in the reflecting pools. This visual lightness was made possible by some heavy engineering, with several hidden transfer structures directing the building's weight down to its foundations. The most significant of these transfer structures is the first-floor slab, whose supporting columns are tucked far back from its edges to hide visible connections between hull and ground. The slab functions like an immense concrete table, with the black steel frames of the upper floors resting upon its edges so that their interiors can remain relatively column-free. To enable the slab to transfer these massive forces, it had to be over a metre thick in places and reinforced with no fewer than 50 steel I-beams, in addition to conventional reinforcement bars. The 'table legs' were engineered to match, with the largest being fabricated from 8 steel beams welded together to take the 2,000-ton force generated by the cantilevered prows of the hulls.

With the hulls' black steelwork in progress, the supporting role of the table-like first-floor slab can be clearly seen. The wish to float the hulls' prows out above the plaza required a dense mesh of steel reinforcement to be buried in the slab, while the see-saw effect of the cantilever placed some of the 'table legs' under compression and others in tension, requiring different sets of calculations.

Soon to be caged within masses of structural steel, the four irregular concrete cores and the massive first-floor slab provided the springboard from which the dynamic hull forms could leap. This combination of concrete and steel offered the best balance between budget and buildability within the tight construction schedule.

The four cores

At the heart of each of the four hulls are the concrete stair cores that rise up from basement level, through the first-floor slab and the rest of the building, to serve the banqueting suite on the fifth floor. The combination of the outward-leaning hull faces and the cores being divided by the open central atrium presented a challenge for RPS's engineers. Each sloping core would have to be capable of supporting itself throughout much of the construction, until the moment when they could be securely tied together by the steel of the banqueting-hall floor, which would bridge the atrium. The risk was that these cores might begin to splay outwards in the interim, under the pressure of their own growing weight or because of strong winds on the exposed site. As a consequence, a great deal of care went into the cores' design, with each being planned as an independent structure to allow it to exist in temporary isolation before being absorbed into the whole.

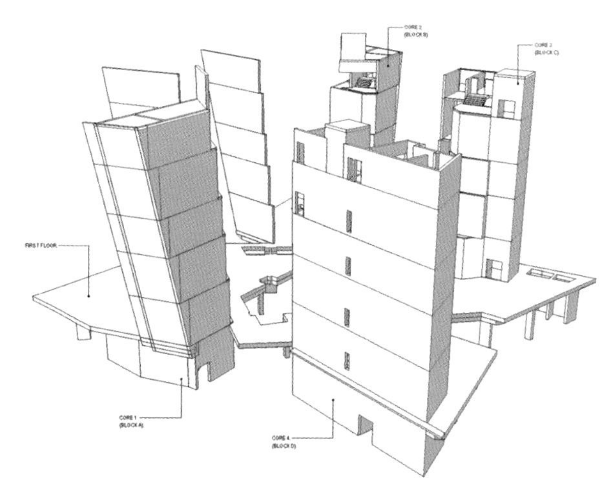

Steel frames

Time being of the essence, Harcourt took the decision to revise the original site work schedule, changing the build plan of Titanic Belfast from a floor-by-floor to a core-by-core sequence. This allowed the different teams to work simultaneously in the tight confines onsite, with steel fabricators following in the footsteps of concrete pourers as each stair core was completed to fifth-floor height. It was the addition of this black steel grid that brought the building to life, with its direct parallels to the shipyard process of attaching ranks of tall frames to the keel to create the profile of the hull. The contrast between concrete and steel also served to emphasise the role of the cantilevered first-floor slab, with the four floating black bows now mimicking archive images of *Titanic*'s own hull as it projected out beyond her stack of keel blocks. Part of the motivation for this break between ground and structure was to avoid creating visual barriers around the building's perimeter that might discourage visitors from circulating freely between the atrium and the surrounding landscape.

Though originally specified as laser-welded steel, the columns were eventually manufactured by hand by Fisher Engineering in County Fermanagh. Fisher's fabricators were able to produce a sharp, crisp finish using the square cut edge of the plate as their guide. Taking weeks to complete the job, the steel fixers had to crawl inside the hollow columns, working in similarly confined spaces as the riveters who fashioned *Titanic*'s double-bottomed hull.

Flying mega-columns

Arguably the most impressive individual elements of the internal structure are the four giant mega-columns that directly support the floor of the banqueting hall. Deliberately echoing the faceted forms of the external cladding, Todd Architects detailed these tall supports with an elegant trapezoid section, so they appear like tall blades of steel slicing through the void. Fabricated as one piece from 20-millimetre-thick steel plate, each of the columns is 25 metres long and weighs around 18 tons. They required the services of a specialised 500-ton crane to lift them dramatically into place. Once securely bolted to the ground-floor slab, the hollow columns were filled with concrete to further enhance their load-bearing capacity. Simply painted black and left undisguised for all to see, the mega-columns possess a solidity and scale on a par with the former products of the shipyard.

A silver sea

The stark silhouettes of the black hull frames did not remain bare for long. As each was completed in sequence, it was quickly sheathed in large white panels of phenolic insulation sandwiched between thin sheets of steel. With a grid of vertical steel rails installed across the white sloping faces, the process of plating the hulls could now begin. Fretted and folded from single sheets of two-millimetre-thick aluminium, the panels measure four metres across the length of their diagonal ridges, which rise and fall according to how their four sides taper. As the four asymmetrical hulls all lean out at different angles, each of the eight facades possesses a unique geometry. To customise the panels to each facade, the angles of the short sides of the trapezoid form were adjusted to match the angle of the relevant bow's leading edge. Wherever a panel met an edge, it had to be cut to fit, requiring approximately 2,000 unique panels to be fabricated. For this reason, every one of the 3,000 panels in the facade had a precisely defined location.

Making the hulls weathertight for the first time, the internal skin of insulating panels brought a renewed resemblance to the early white card concept models through which CivicArts had evolved the form.

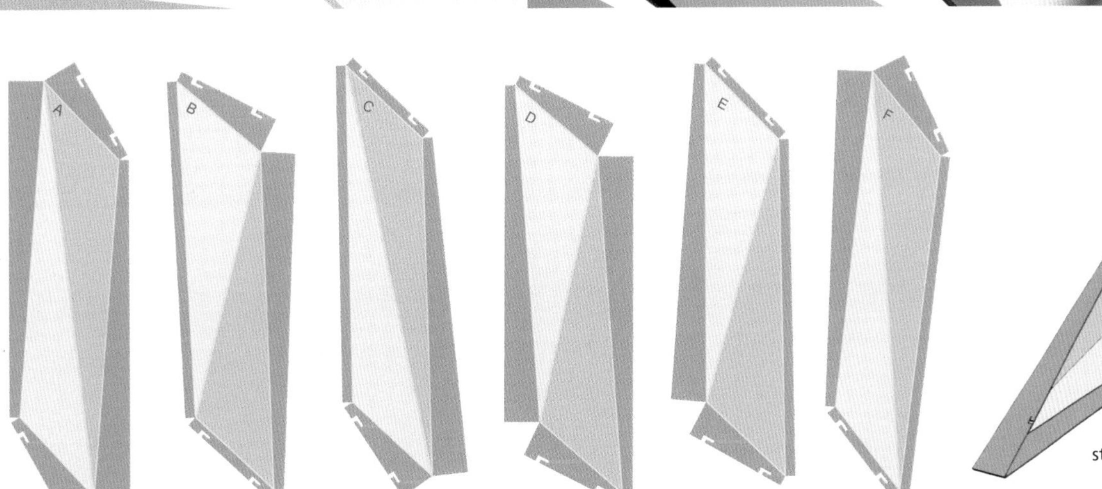

To create the random cut-diamond pattern of an abstract seascape, each of the eight facades was composed of six different panel patterns, none of which was repeated more than twenty times. Multiplied over the eight facades, each with a different angle to its prow, this created forty-eight different panel styles to be manufactured, excluding the customised edge components.

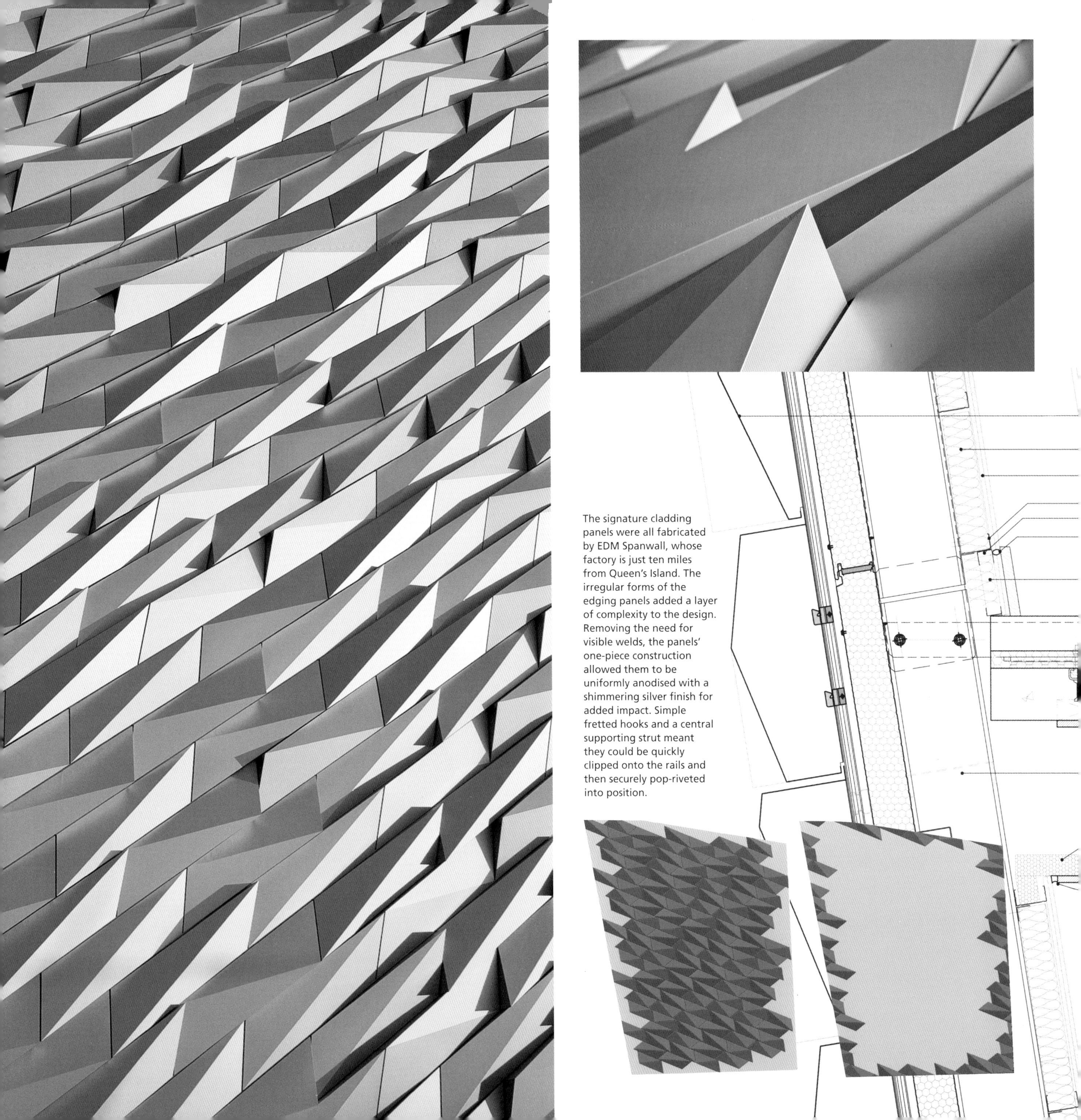

The signature cladding panels were all fabricated by EDM Spanwall, whose factory is just ten miles from Queen's Island. The irregular forms of the edging panels added a layer of complexity to the design. Removing the need for visible welds, the panels' one-piece construction allowed them to be uniformly anodised with a shimmering silver finish for added impact. Simple fretted hooks and a central supporting strut meant they could be quickly clipped onto the rails and then securely pop-riveted into position.

KOMAT

A room with a view

With the connection between building and context being of prime importance, every effort was made to maximise views out through the tall, glazed, central 'crystal', especially where it aligned with the historic slipways. This underlying motivation led to an intelligent piece of engineering, not readily apparent to the casual observer. The tall, slender steel mullions that divide the glazing panels are in fact load-bearing elements, every bit as structurally essential as the black steel frames of the hulls to either side.

As well as carrying a considerable weight of glass, these vertical elements support the pointed outer edges of the floor plates, leaving these panoramic viewing platforms free of columns for easy circulation. Shifting these structural members to the platforms' edges meant the stunning views out towards the river could be unobtrusively framed. Originally designed as hollow box sections, it was contractor Metallbau Früh who proposed laser-cutting the mullions from solid 300-by-70-millimetre steel bars. Like the crisply fabricated mega-columns, this weight of metal gives the mullions a satisfying solidity.

Temporary red-painted steel columns were used to support the structure until the final mullions were fully installed and ready to take the load. Cutting directly through the central line of sight, these obstructive red steel pillars neatly illustrate the kind of structural elements that the elegant mullion solution was able to avoid.

Metallbau Früh also manufactured the large double-glazed panels that afford such fine clear views down the historic slipways. Their laminated construction combines a toughened outer layer with various inner-surface treatments, including solar control and other special coatings, which moderate the UV light coming in during the summer, while helping retain heat during the winter months.

Like a surrealist composition of floating oblong forms, the elements of these disembodied escalators were suspended in mid-air before being carefully connected to each other to form a solid single stair.

Atrium activity

With the glazing in place, and the building watertight work could get under way on the Great Atrium that would form the beating heart of Titanic Belfast. Some of the most impressive engineering elements in this lofty space are the escalators that whisk visitors across the void, taking them from the ground to the galleries or on to the banqueting suites above. Prefabricated in sections by leading manufacturer Kone, the longest of these dynamic steel diagonals measures just under 25 metres in length with 124 steps, making it the longest free-span escalator in the whole of Ireland. Installing these giants was a delicate operation, with the sections being brought in at ground level, then hoisted to the appropriate floor before being swung out and coupled *in situ*. Temporary steelwork had to be installed to support a web of block and tackle that allowed workers to position these massive components with precision as they dangled from the ceiling.

The atrium's intended parallels with the Arrol Gantry were dramatically brought to life as the fit-out progressed, presenting a contemporary reincarnation of the workspace between *Titanic*'s and *Olympic*'s hulls. The towers of temporary scaffolding stood in for the gantry's stanchions, with the diminutive figures of workmen offering a tangible sense of scale as they hung the individual plates of the rusted feature wall upon its contoured frame of rails.

The lower beam of the Vierendeel truss lies buried within the mezzanine floor, occupying the point of the diamond plan nearest the slipways. Highlighted in red within the computer model, the truss's central structural role within the forest of roof beams is easy to discern. Images of it in the early phases of installation also recall its original design intent – as a tool for bridging the many canals and rivers of Belgium.

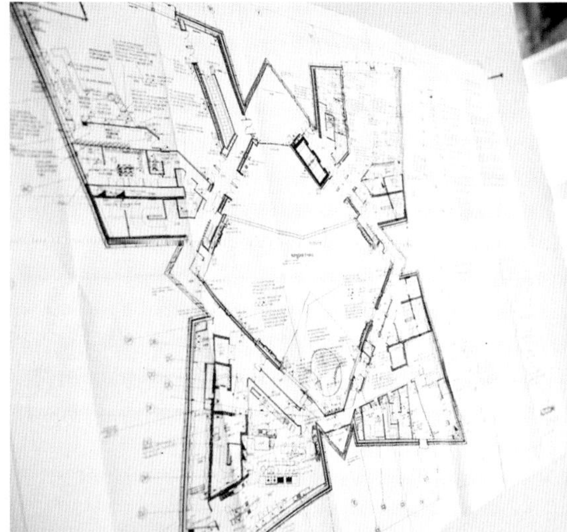

Beam above the banqueters

Conceived as one of Belfast's grandest rooms, the uninterrupted sweep of the banqueting hall's roof is supported by an engineering solution even older than *Titanic* herself. The Vierendeel truss was invented in 1895 by a Belgian civil engineer, Arthur Vierendeel, and first employed in a bridge he built in 1902. The significant feature of the truss's design is that it dispenses with the usual diagonal bracing between vertical elements. Instead, it relies for its strength upon the rigid connections and more substantial construction of its rectangular frames. This leaves clear, straight-sided openings between its verticals, and it is through these empty frames that guests on the mezzanine now mingle, unaware of the hidden ring of steel around them. With its ends resting on metre-deep sections of steel girder, the load-bearing properties of this 30-metre truss allow it to bridge the gap between two concrete cores, permitting the Titanic Suite to remain pillarless. The resulting events space measures over 800 square metres and is capable of seating 580 diners, or as many as 750 guests arranged theatre-style to listen to speakers address them from the Grand Staircase.

Designed by Kay Elliott, the fluted wooden columns on the mezzanine disguise the steel verticals of the massive Vierendeel truss that carries the weight of the roof. Similar techniques were deployed aboard Edwardian liners, where steel masts penetrating down through the decks were discreetly incorporated into the décor of the restaurants and salons by means of paint effects or wooden panelling.

All hands on deck

The 12 months between March 2011 and March 2012 saw an army of workmen swarm around inside the hulls of Titanic Belfast, readying the building for the symbolic opening date. Like *Titanic* herself, this multi-faceted visitor destination would require a myriad of skills to complete her fit-out – from joiners and plasterers to electricians and plumbers – all working in close proximity within the confines of the building's compact footprint. The strict time constraints imposed by the building schedule meant that much of the structural steelwork had to be designed and ordered before the mechanical services were finalised. This created a fixed three-dimensional labyrinth of floors and beams through which building-services engineers AECOM were obliged to thread the final configuration of pipes and ducts. Dimly lit by bare strip-lights, the shadowy plant rooms from which these pipes snaked began to resemble images of *Titanic*'s own engine rooms, as they slowly filled with machinery to pump hot water, extract cooking fumes and circulate fresh air.

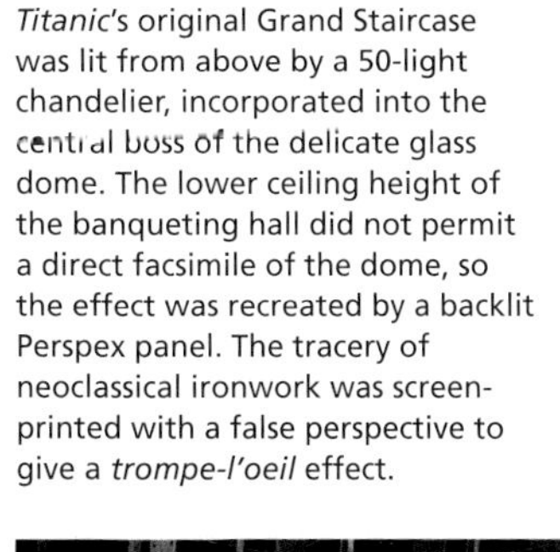

Titanic's original Grand Staircase was lit from above by a 50-light chandelier, incorporated into the central boss of the delicate glass dome. The lower ceiling height of the banqueting hall did not permit a direct facsimile of the dome, so the effect was recreated by a backlit Perspex panel. The tracery of neoclassical ironwork was screen-printed with a false perspective to give a *trompe-l'oeil* effect.

Back above the waterline, the job of partitioning the echoing hulls advanced at speed, with workers lining and subdividing the insulated steel frames to create the shop, restaurants, galleries and event spaces that would soon be filled with guests. Like a site within a site, the fit-out of Gallery 2's shipyard ride began to mirror the activity around it, as Paragon Creative's craftsmen recreated the island works of Harland & Wolff, complete with full-sized facsimiles of *Titanic*'s components amidst the Arrol Gantry. High above them in the busy banqueting hall, the finishing touches were being made to the stately Grand Staircase beneath its patterned Perspex dome. Emerging from its cocoon of dust-sheets and scaffolding, its warm oak hues would provide a polished reminder of the finely finished products that once sailed from these yards.

Diamond in the rough

The year 2012 dawned to find Titanic Belfast just weeks away from completion. Always calculated as a three-year build, the project would be finished on time and on budget thanks to the raft of architects, engineers and consultants who had poured so much creativity and ingenuity into this complex composition. With its eight dynamic diamond facades reflecting the ever-changing skies, this precious cut-and-polished object stood set in splendid isolation upon the raw earth of the reclaimed shipyard. It was a contrast as marked as that between the grit of the original working shipyards and the glamour of the luxurious liners they once forged. Now began the final push to finish the internal fit-out and complete the external landscaping that would make this the ultimate *Titanic* visitor attraction. This was to be the year when Titanic Belfast welcomed the world through its doors.

H&W

#4
BULKHEADS AND DECKING
There were 15 watertight bulkheads that ran across Titanic in the lower decks. These divided the ship's hull into 16 watertight compartments.
ORDINARY DOORS SUCH AS THOSE IN MOST PASSENGER AREAS WERE A POINT OF WEAKNESS.
TITANIC'S INTERNAL STRUCTURE
The bulkheads were connected to the shell plating. The collision bulkhead was located at the bow of the ship and fitted to be an inner watertight skin should the bow be damaged in an end on collision.

Crafting an experience

Titanic Belfast is not a museum, but an experience. Different from a book, a film or a TV series, but managing to contain elements of each, it has a quality all of its own. Conventional museums are largely object based, with cabinets of labelled artefacts to convey information. On Queen's Island, however, there was no such collection to be housed. But there was a story to be told.

Event Communications are storytellers first, designers second. Their work flows from the narrative they form, and every project is unique because every story is different. Event are perhaps unique in having an in-house interpretive team who gathered the material, defined the narrative arc and wrote a brief that could be returned to throughout the process, to ensure the core message was being conveyed. There was a clear genealogy at work, where the storyline could be seen to structure the experience. Collaborating with researchers, interpreters and local sources, the story that emerged was one of Belfast in all her diversity. This was a city whose wealth from engineering, trade and linen allowed her to fund both great ships and great buildings. Though by no means the only ship to be launched into the River Lagan, *Titanic* was a defining product of her age and an icon in maritime history. The story of her making had never been told in great detail, but here was the natural backdrop for that narrative. The shipyard site itself is effectively a historic artefact in the round, providing unparalleled authenticity with its industrial *genius loci.* In crafting their galleries with the city's story as their guide, Event would build an attraction that was unique to Belfast.

From the gantry to the galleries

Like the jagged building they inhabit, the galleries of Titanic Belfast went through a long and detailed development, with Event involved from the outset. The earliest proposals date back to 2004, when Event became part of the Titanic Signature Project Team. Exploring ideas for a cultural attraction on Queen's Island, the team selected the original slipways as their site, with a concept that shared both the form and footprint of the mighty Arrol Gantry. To fill a portion of this massive oblong volume, Event proposed a dramatic installation that would have been one of the largest models in the world. Scaled at almost 1:25, it aimed to recreate the hull of *Titanic* under construction, lying beside that of *Olympic* approaching completion – just as the yard would have appeared before *Olympic*'s launch in 1910. The idea of experiencing the yards in three dimensions would remain consistent throughout the project's development, as would the wider narrative arc that always embedded *Titanic* within the context of the bustling city that helped shape her.

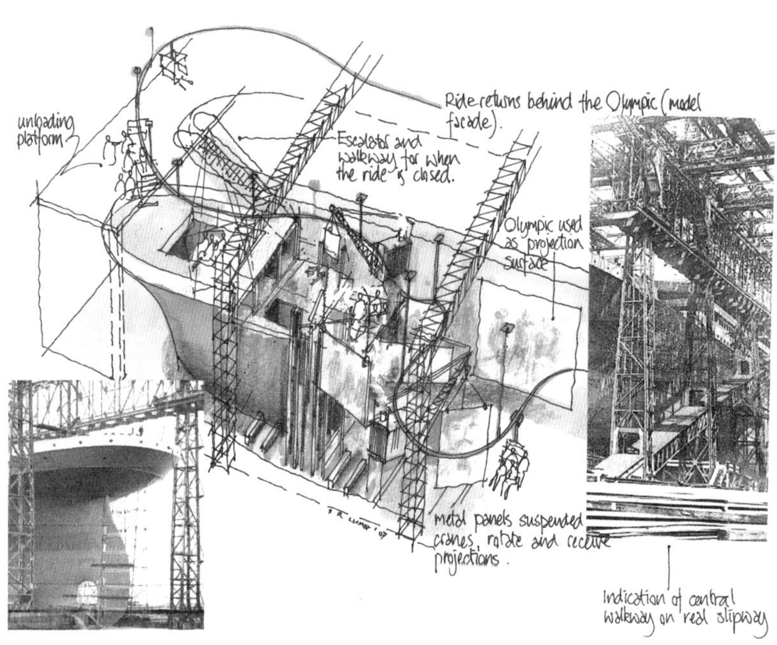

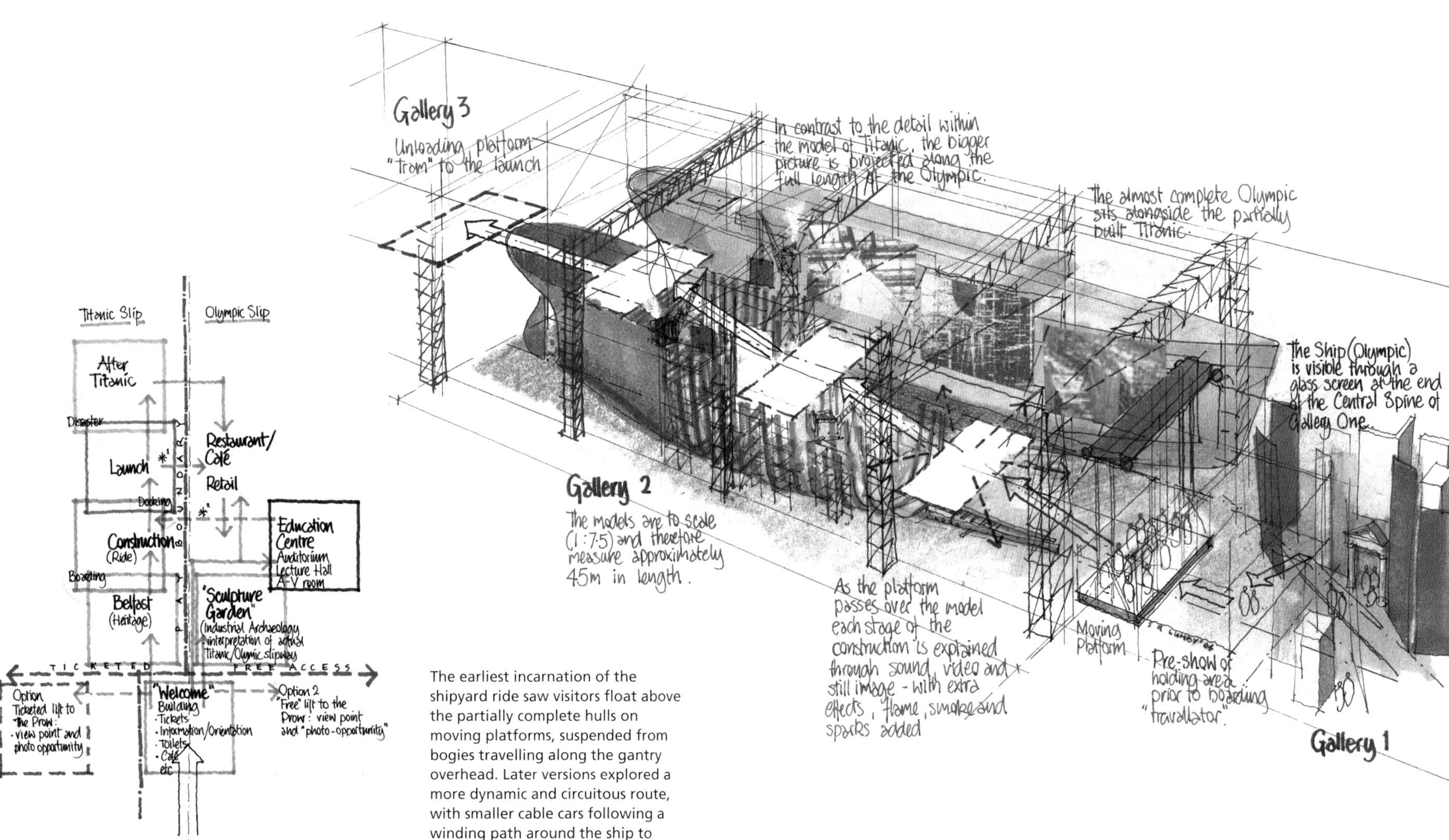

The earliest incarnation of the shipyard ride saw visitors float above the partially complete hulls on moving platforms, suspended from bogies travelling along the gantry overhead. Later versions explored a more dynamic and circuitous route, with smaller cable cars following a winding path around the ship to gain different dramatic perspectives.

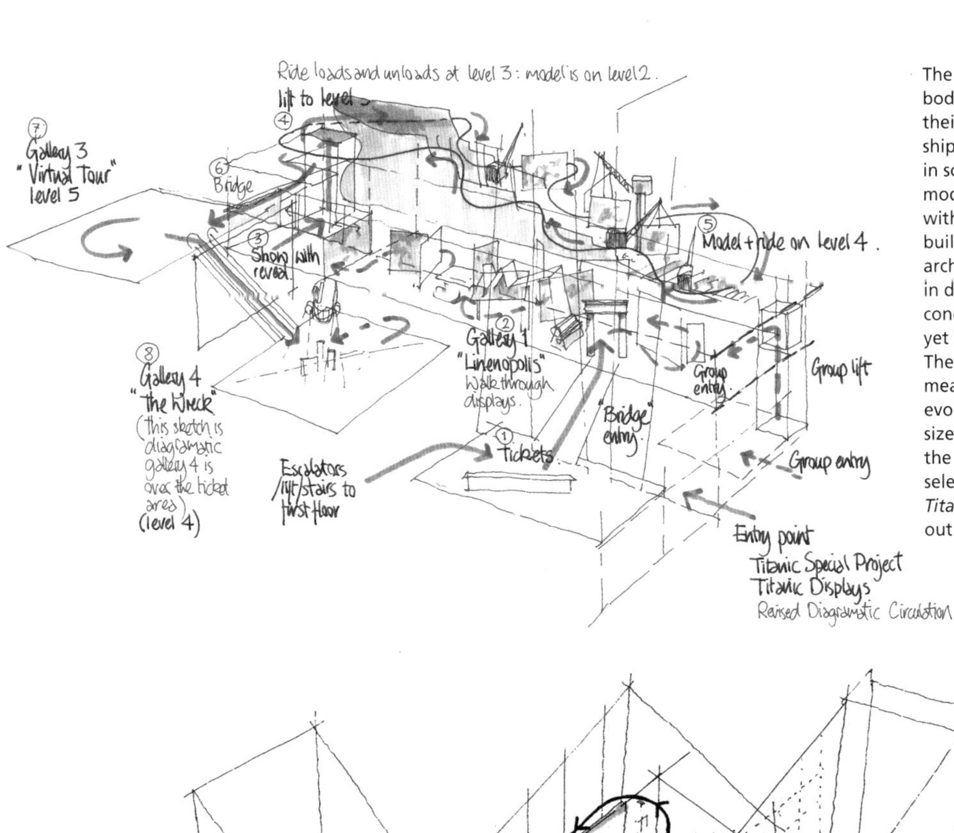

The project's shift from the body of the slipways to their head required the shipyard ride to be reduced in scale, as the two ship models now had to fit within two hulls of the building. As the architecture was developed in detail, the expanding concrete cores encroached yet further on the galleries. These space constraints meant that the ship models evolved into tangible full-sized ship components for the ride's scenery, with selected portions of *Titanic*'s hull now looming out of the dark.

The narrative power of the shipyard ride ensured its survival through the radical changes to the building's architecture. A close collaboration formed, with Event and CivicArts considering the impact of each design evolution on the internal spaces through which *Titanic*'s tale would be woven. The storyline that emerged from Event's researchers required nine galleries, arranged in sequence like a theatrical promenade, demanding a continuous circulation pattern occupying multiple levels. The complexity of the building's geometry and the demands of building regulations made this a game of architectural Tetris for CivicArts and Todd Architects, but the final configuration of irregular voids forged exciting internal spaces. Though Event's final design utilises the full spectrum of presentation techniques, from traditional static models to interactive displays, technology is never used for its own sake, but applied only when appropriate to convey the story with clarity. The richness of that story is matched by the manner of its telling – in Titanic Belfast's galleries, content is king.

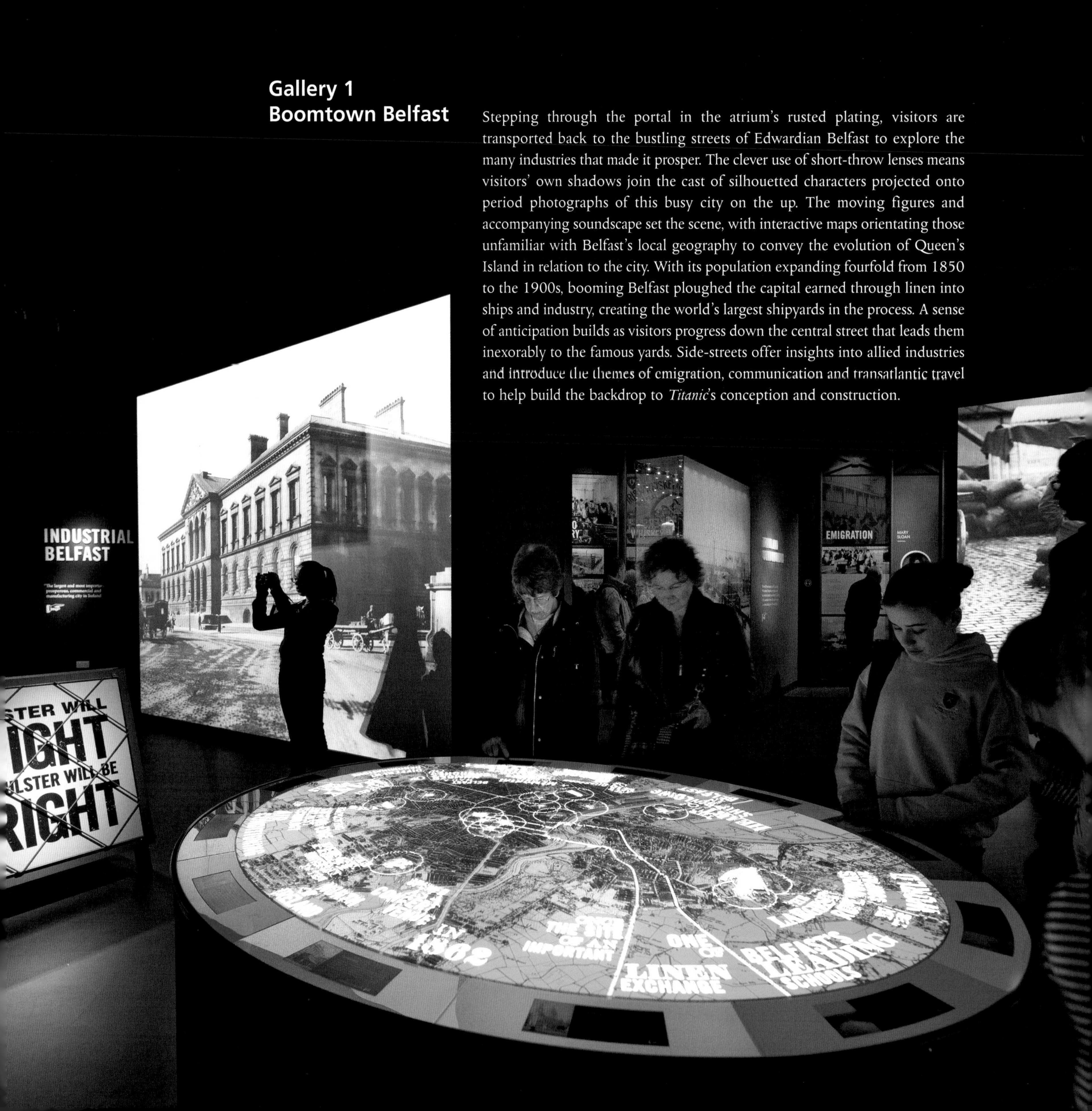

Gallery 1
Boomtown Belfast

Stepping through the portal in the atrium's rusted plating, visitors are transported back to the bustling streets of Edwardian Belfast to explore the many industries that made it prosper. The clever use of short-throw lenses means visitors' own shadows join the cast of silhouetted characters projected onto period photographs of this busy city on the up. The moving figures and accompanying soundscape set the scene, with interactive maps orientating those unfamiliar with Belfast's local geography to convey the evolution of Queen's Island in relation to the city. With its population expanding fourfold from 1850 to the 1900s, booming Belfast ploughed the capital earned through linen into ships and industry, creating the world's largest shipyards in the process. A sense of anticipation builds as visitors progress down the central street that leads them inexorably to the famous yards. Side-streets offer insights into allied industries and introduce the themes of emigration, communication and transatlantic travel to help build the backdrop to *Titanic*'s conception and construction.

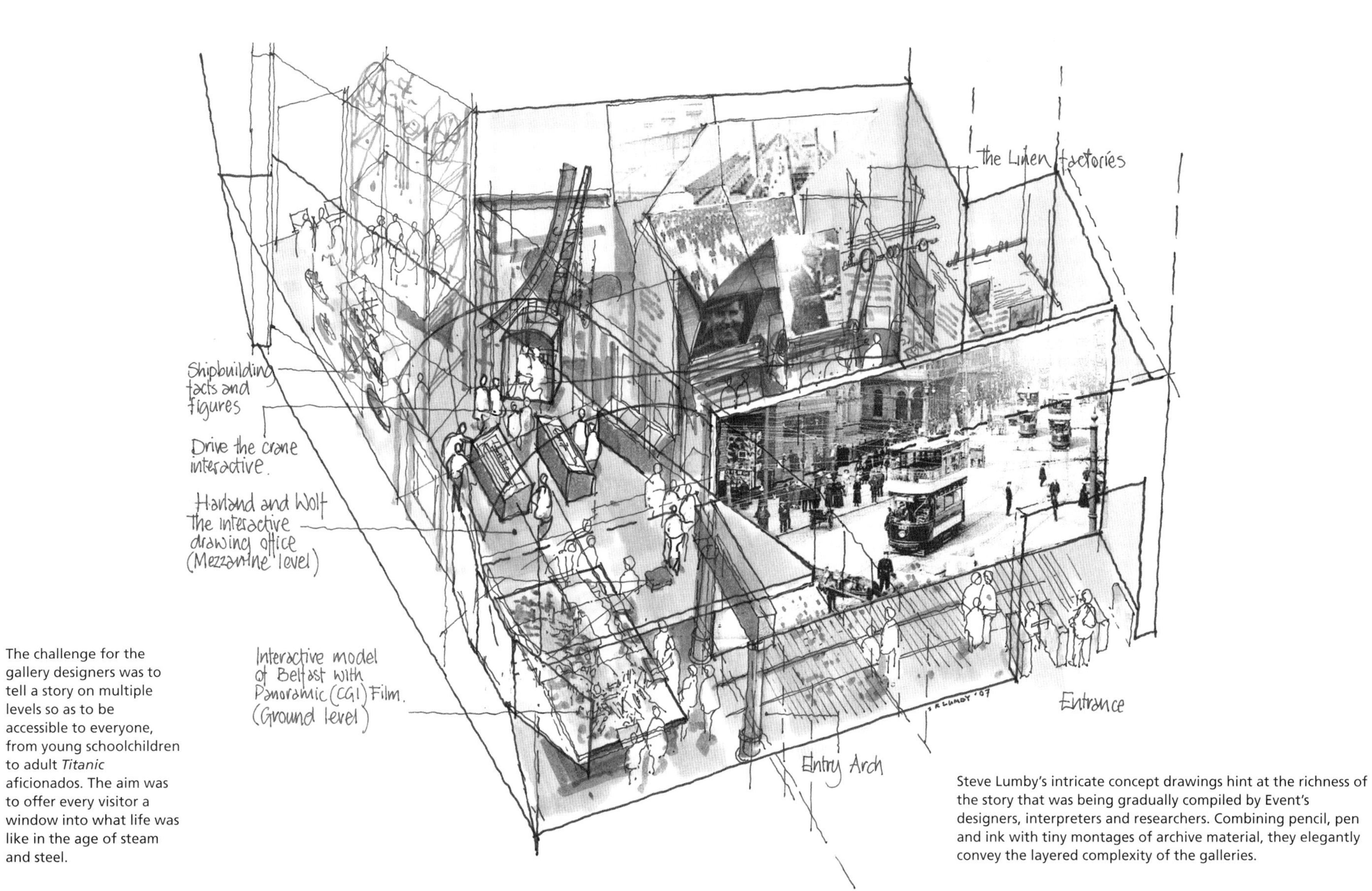

The challenge for the gallery designers was to tell a story on multiple levels so as to be accessible to everyone, from young schoolchildren to adult *Titanic* aficionados. The aim was to offer every visitor a window into what life was like in the age of steam and steel.

Steve Lumby's intricate concept drawings hint at the richness of the story that was being gradually compiled by Event's designers, interpreters and researchers. Combining pencil, pen and ink with tiny montages of archive material, they elegantly convey the layered complexity of the galleries.

Putting the commissioning of *Titanic* into context, the displays built a graphic picture of the British and American rivalry that drove the construction of ever-bigger and ever-better ships. The narrative addresses those at every level of society, from the captains of industry to the workforce that laboured under them, representing every class to be found amongst passengers and crew.

Gallery 2
The Shipyard

An original pair of the old yard's iron gates provides an authentic threshold to the world of Harland & Wolff. The gallery's initial emphasis is on the white-collar workers and the immense amount of planning and preparation that went into the *Olympic*-class liners before a single rivet had been struck. Visitors enter a representation of the drawing offices, where projectors cause a mass of technical drawings to scroll across the floor and walls, like plans rolled out across a draughting table. Selectively highlighting and animating machine components makes the blueprints to come to life, conveying the inner workings of the ships, complete with sound effects. Like the draughtsmen in the original drawing offices, visitors can hear echoes of the riveters from the galleries above – a reminder of the close proximity of those conceiving and constructing these immense liners. A later series of interactive screens compiles and animates the plans and elevations taking visitors through the construction process step by step.

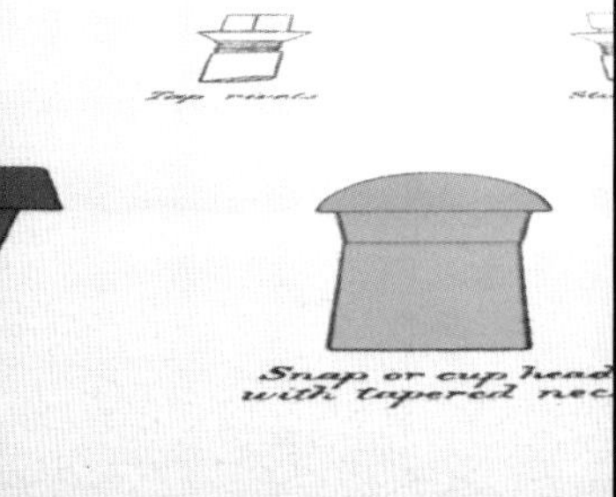

The floor has a major interactive element, with light sensors capable of following a person's footfall. Whole families can play the rivets game, frenetically stamping rivets into hull plates against the clock. They can also play spot the difference with the many types of rivet used to join different surfaces of the ship. Accompanied by sound effects, the animated drawings convey the blur of turbine blades and the pulsing force of the ship's colossal reciprocating pistons.

The shipyard ride

Leaving the bright projections of the drawing offices behind, visitors enter a dark, atmospheric void and ascend a recreation of the mighty Arrol Gantry in an industrial cage lift. Here, high amongst the gantry's beams and girders, they are surrounded by images of men at work, joining immense steel plates with hammers and hydraulic riveting machines. The gantry forms the dramatic approach to the galleries' theatrical centrepiece – the long-envisaged aerial shipyard ride. Here visitors board two-tier cars, suspended from a winding ceiling track on scissor lifts, then begin their twisting descent into the steam, smoke and smells of the Edwardian shipyard. The ride provides visitors with a tangible sense of *Titanic*'s unprecedented scale through its full-sized partial reconstructions of her bow and stern. The ride format was deliberately chosen as a means of changing guests' perspective, focusing their attention on key moments in the construction narrative, which are relayed via video screens strategically embedded in the scenic reconstructions.

Standing beneath the aerial ride during a preview event, this journalist is dwarfed by Paragon's reconstruction of *Titanic*'s rudder, hanging on its massive gudgeons. Standing nine metres tall, this element reveals only a fraction of the ship's true bulk – it stood as high as a nine-storey building.

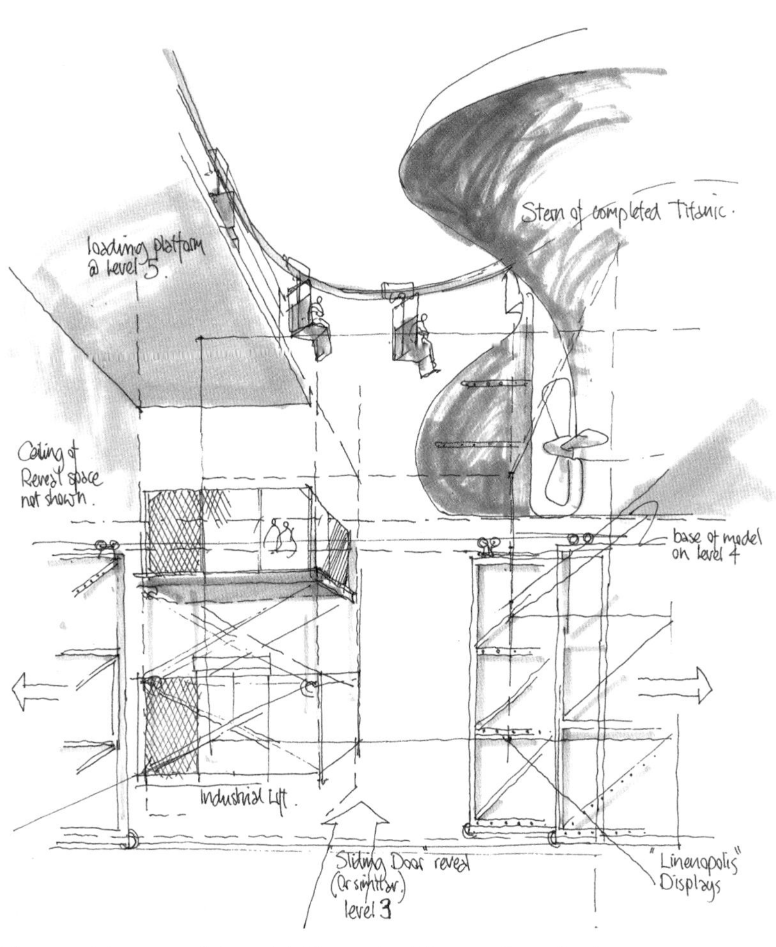

The essential concept of the aerial ride remained the same throughout its development, differing only in the scale and extent of the hull the cars were to sail over. Early ideas included a theatrical staggered approach, with groups admitted through sliding doors, then raised to mount the ride via an open scissor lift.

The dizzying height of the Arrol Gantry lift shaft is a reminder of the dangerous conditions in which shipbuilders laboured, with the ever-present risk of falling from the scaffold or being struck by tools or materials dropped from above.

THE LAUNCH

'She took to the water as though she were eager for the baptism.'

Gallery 3
The Launch

Leaving Gallery 2, visitors emerge from the gloom of the gritty shipyards to be greeted by the sounds of a wildly cheering crowd, mingling with the pomp of a patriotic brass band. Stepping into the natural light, they find themselves in a triangular room, glazed from floor to ceiling, on which an image of *Titanic* lying on the slipway has been applied. The crowd's cheers rise as a central video monitor plays archive footage of *Olympic*'s launch. As the white-painted hull takes to the water, the opaque image of her sister ship magically dissolves to reveal a commanding view down the very same slipway as it appears today. The glass's special electro-sensitive film allows this theatrical demonstration to be performed continuously throughout the day. Making full use of the building's deliberate alignment, this site-specific installation illustrates the unparalleled authenticity of Titanic Belfast and its Queen's Island site for the retelling of *Titanic*'s story.

The massive chains filling the prow of the panoramic viewing platform are a reminder of the great weight of metal that was being put in motion. *Titanic*'s descent down the slipway was a carefully managed exercise, with many tons of lubricant to ease her way and chains to arrest her motion, preventing her from striking the opposite bank.

Sketch view of G3 with revised location of central monitor. (Glazing showing revealed state). Nov. 2011 (Not to scale).

An estimated 100,000 people witnessed *Titanic*'s launch, equivalent to a third of the city's Edwardian population. The designers carefully aligned the applied image on the glass with the angle of the archive footage and the vantage point afforded by the panoramic balcony to create a dramatic simulation of that momentous event of 31st May 1911.

Gallery 4
Fit-Out

When she first took to the water on that day in May, *Titanic* was nothing but an empty hull. Within an hour she had been towed to the deep-water wharf, where the long fit-out could begin. The fit-out gallery opens with a large divided model of the ship in the process of receiving its heavy machinery, with companion displays detailing the weight of boilers, engines, flues and funnels that would power it across the Atlantic. Rounding the corner, visitors are greeted by detailed full-sized reconstructions of the different cabins that celebrate the fine craftsmanship of Harland & Wolff's joiners, upholsterers and decorators. With the outer cabin walls entirely glazed, visitors have clear views of all the cabin fittings, from the luxurious first-class Staterooms and well-appointed second-class quarters to the modest third-class accommodation. Rejecting static costumed mannequins, Event brought these cabin sets to life by creating ghostly projected characters of *Titanic*'s passengers, who can be heard conversing with each other as they explore their sleeping quarters.

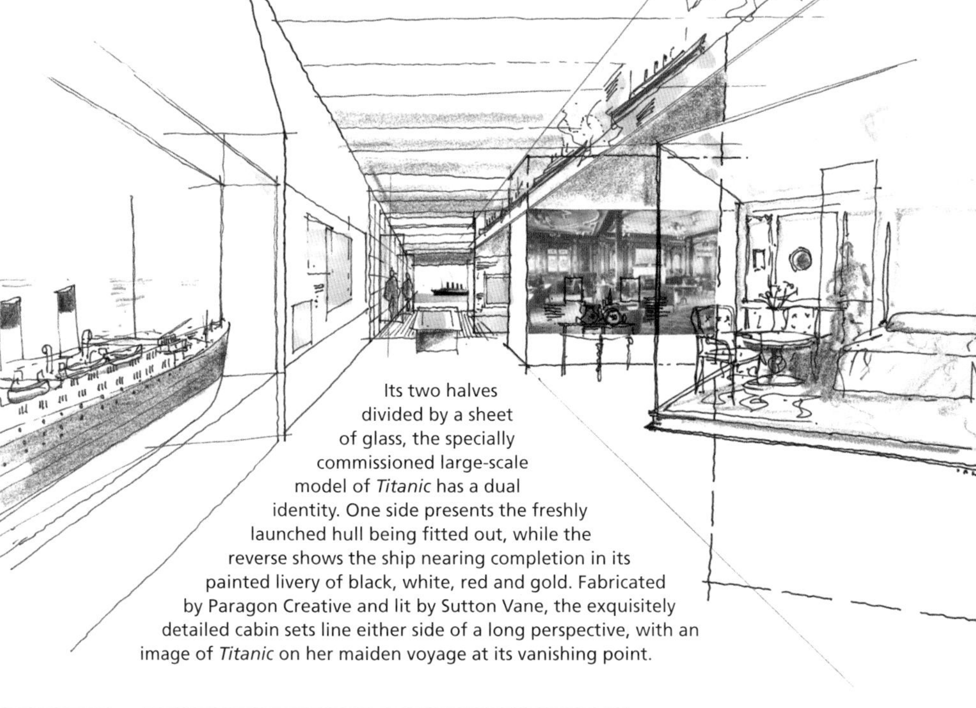

Its two halves divided by a sheet of glass, the specially commissioned large-scale model of *Titanic* has a dual identity. One side presents the freshly launched hull being fitted out, while the reverse shows the ship nearing completion in its painted livery of black, white, red and gold. Fabricated by Paragon Creative and lit by Sutton Vane, the exquisitely detailed cabin sets line either side of a long perspective, with an image of *Titanic* on her maiden voyage at its vanishing point.

The gallery's central attraction is the 'Cave', a dynamic virtual environment whose three-screen all-round projections whisk visitors on a vertical journey through the ship's stacked decks. Beginning in the engine room, the film takes full advantage of the near-seamless transition between the rear projection screens, allowing the camera to pan steadily around the rooms. Though the famous Grand Staircase could not be made to fit within the galleries, it can still be explored here in virtual form.

Gallery 5
Maiden Voyage

A moment of calm before the calamity ahead, the fifth gallery documents *Titanic*'s maiden voyage, with its simple evocation of her upper decks. The natural lighting, timber floors and replica benches set the scene, while glass partitions carry life-sized enlargements from Fr Francis Browne's famous photographs, so that visitors may walk shoulder to shoulder past *Titanic*'s passengers. Fr Browne was saved only because his superior ordered him to disembark at Queenstown, and his images remain a poignant record of life on board just three days before the fateful collision with the iceberg. A series of wall panels documents *Titanic*'s itinerary and the growing quantities of passengers and provisions that were loaded onto the ship in each successive port, including the Guarantee Group under Harland & Wolff's young Chief Designer, Thomas Andrews. The final image along the back wall shows *Titanic* preparing to depart from Queenstown and head out into the cold Atlantic on the afternoon of 11th April 1911.

Gallery 6 The Sinking

Leaving the light-filled decks behind, visitors are plunged into darkness as the moment of *Titanic*'s sinking draws near. Event took a deliberately understated approach to this pivotal point in the narrative, seeking a reflective tone that would avoid sensationalising the tragic loss of over 1,500 lives. A thoughtful counterpoint to the epic spectacles of existing Hollywood dramas, the gallery shifts the visitor's focus away from the moment of impact (which very few witnessed), to the slow, seeping sense of panic amongst passengers and crew as it dawned on them that the 'unsinkable' ship was doomed to disappear beneath the waves. There were to be no refrigerated icebergs or literal dramatic reconstructions of the hull being torn in two. Instead, a soundscape of compelling first-hand testimonies would convey the human emotions of those calamitous two-and-a-half hours between the iceberg being struck and ship slipping from sight. The drama lies in the tales of sleepy passengers being awoken in the dead of night and confronted with a fight for survival.

The angular, jutting walls of the winding passage to the sinking were an integral part of the dark, disorientating environment Event wished to create. The complex faceted surfaces proved impossible to draw in two dimensions and had to be fabricated entirely by eye by the galleries' skilled team of plasterers. Across them scroll the Morse-code distress signals sent by *Titanic*'s Marconi wireless operators, trying to alert the world to the unfolding tragedy.

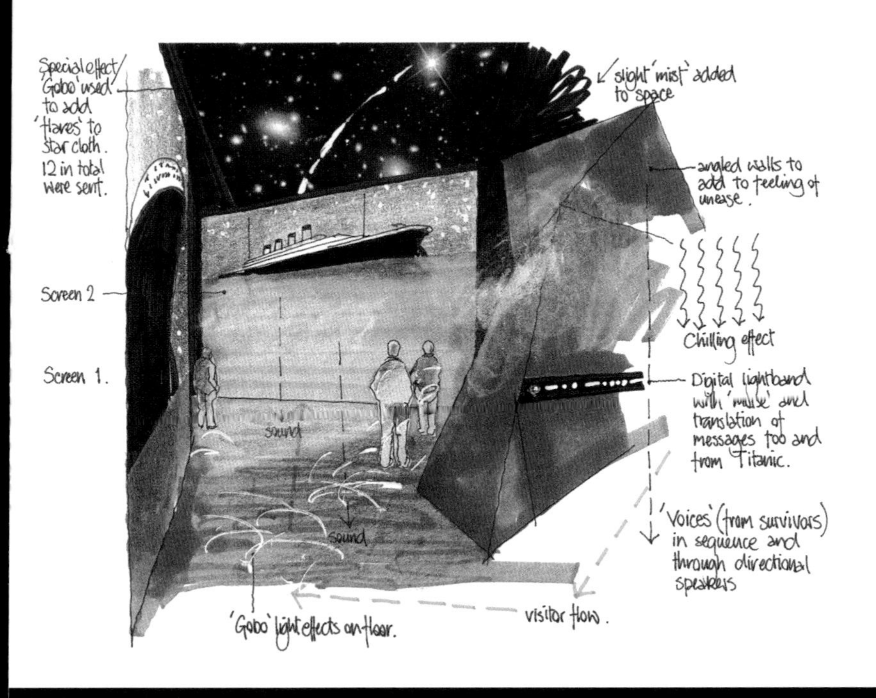

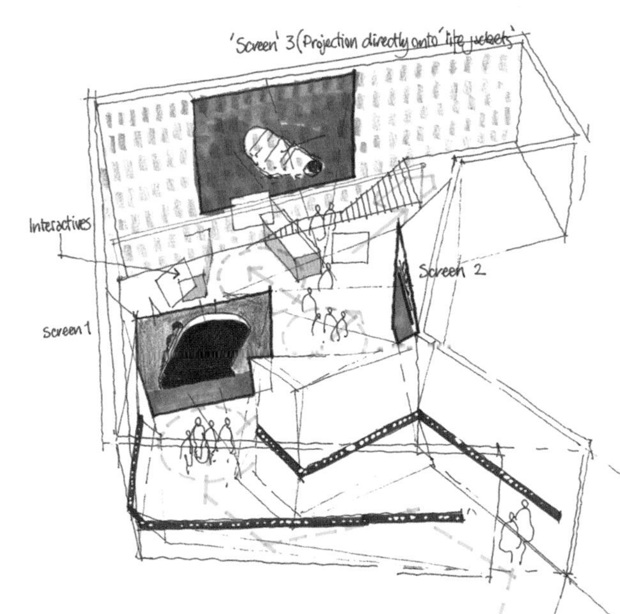

The gallery was planned as a series of pools of light and sound to guide visitors through events in series. The dark intensity of the space was to be accompanied by a drop in temperature, evoking the vast, cold, eerie North Atlantic silence that engulfed the survivors in the lifeboats once the ship had slipped beneath the surface.

Event chose to record the sinking through traditional animation as opposed to modern computer graphics, with large period-style depictions showing the sequence of *Titanic*'s final moments. These provide a steady backdrop, allowing visitors to concentrate on the central soundscape that conveys the gallery's main content. The silent darkness of that moonless April night is broken by the staccato sound of distress signals sent in Morse code and the moving oral testimonies of passengers and crew. Pinpricks of fibre-optic light suggest the celestial sweep of the dark northern sky overhead, while floor projections evoke the halo of *Titanic*'s hundreds of blazing electric lights being reflected on the smooth surface of the Atlantic. A range of general sound effects shape the mood of the space, with directional loudspeakers creating spot effects into which visitors walk. Thus the different disembodied voices remain distinct instead of competing for attention. This emphasis on delivering first-hand accounts of that night's events imbues the gallery with greater authenticity than any modern cinematic reconstruction.

Visitors can now learn the fate of the cast of 12 characters whose lives have been tracked in the preceding galleries, with panels recording their last known words or surviving testimonies.

URGENT FULL STEAM

Time 1.40AM Date 15 APRIL 1912

PLEASE TELL YOUR CAPTAIN THIS:

THE OLYMPIC IS MAKING ALL SPEED FOR TITANIC. YOU ARE MUCH NEARER TO TITANIC.

TITANIC IS ALREADY PUTTING WOMEN OFF IN THE BOATS, AND HE SAYS THE WEATHER THERE IS CALM AND CLEAR.

THE OLYMPIC IS THE ONLY SHIP WE HAVE HEARD SAY, "GOING TO THE ASSISTANCE OF TITANIC". THE OTHERS MUST BE A LONG WAY FROM TITANIC'

Reminiscent of the massed ranks of white grave-markers to be found in First World War cemeteries, the wall of stylised cork lifejackets forms a poignant transition between the Sinking and Aftermath galleries, serving as a reminder of the many victims who have no known grave.

'YOU HAVE HAD A LARGE EXPERIENCE OF ICE?'

The British Board of Trade Inquiry was longer and more formal than the American investigation. It relied more on experts than the memories of survivors.

The contrasting red and blue displays highlight the different style and character of the official American and British enquires. The American system gave far greater scope for witness statements from passengers and crew, whereas the British one gave precedence to panels of experts, taking statements from only three passengers, all of them from first class.

Gallery 7
The Aftermath

The massive public outcry prompted by *Titanic*'s sinking demanded an official response, and inquiries were soon being organised on both sides of the Atlantic. In the Aftermath gallery, visitors encounter a full-size replica of one of *Titanic*'s lifeboats, whose insufficient numbers and partial occupation were to be closely scrutinised. The screen above brings the formal proceedings to life, with two actors in period costume delivering dramatic extracts from the official transcripts. Amongst the tales of recrimination, the displays also highlight the positive outcomes of the disaster, such as the new requirements for wirelesses to be manned 24 hours a day and for a ship's lifeboat capacity to be calculated according to its passenger numbers and not its tonnage. The story emphatically extends beyond the immediate aftermath to document the careers of *Titanic*'s sister ships, *Britannic* and *Olympic*, drawing attention to the fact that Belfast's shipbuilding industry continued to forge ahead despite the tragic loss of her most famous product. The yellow crane framing the exit acts as a reminder that Harland & Wolff remain in business to this day.

Always styled as an 'experience' rather than a 'museum', the emphasis of Titanic Belfast's galleries is on atmosphere rather than artefacts. One dramatic exception is the original 33-foot-long plan of *Titanic* used at the British Wreck Commissioner's inquiry into the disaster, which began on 2nd May 1912 and lasted 36 days. Easily read from across the rooms of the London Scottish Drill Hall, the large-scale plan was used as a common point of reference by the 96 witnesses called to give evidence.

Executed in pen and ink, the plan includes marks made during the course of the inquiry, showing the presumed points at which the iceberg holed *Titanic*'s hull. Having been in private hands for decades, this hugely significant artefact sold at auction in May 2011 for £220,000, making it the world's most expensive piece of *Titanic* memorabilia. The owner subsequently agreed to have it placed on public display within Titanic Belfast, where it is now conserved within a specially constructed glass case installed in late 2012.

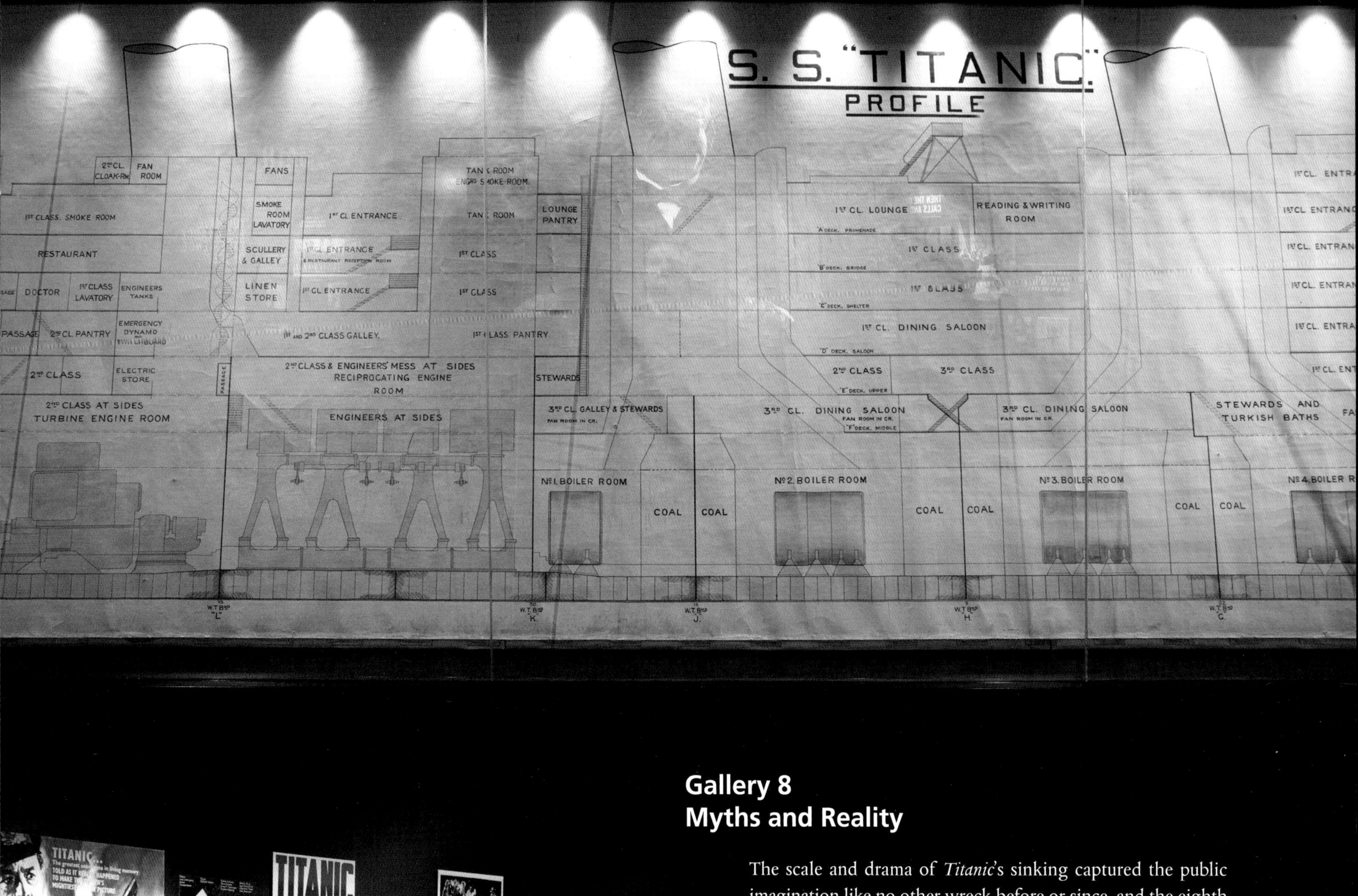

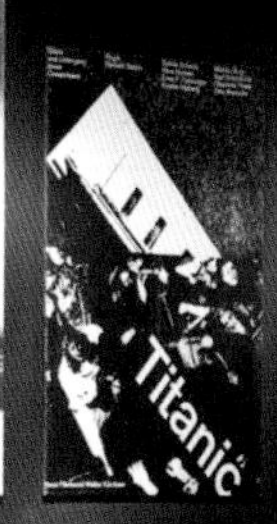

Gallery 8
Myths and Reality

The scale and drama of *Titanic*'s sinking captured the public imagination like no other wreck before or since, and the eighth gallery explores the explosion of ephemera and other cultural manifestations pertaining to the ship and the supposed events aboard. Without the physical evidence to establish the facts, an accretion of myths and legends built up to fill the vacuum. An interactive table enables visitors to explore a selection of the films, books, plays and poetry that *Titanic* has inspired, with objects floating to the surface of a watery background as new conspiracies surface. Visitors' selections from the table help drive the content being projected on a large screen behind them, while additional displays analyse the myths against the now-known facts. It was the power of these stories that fuelled the desire to locate the wreck and finally unlock the ship's secrets.

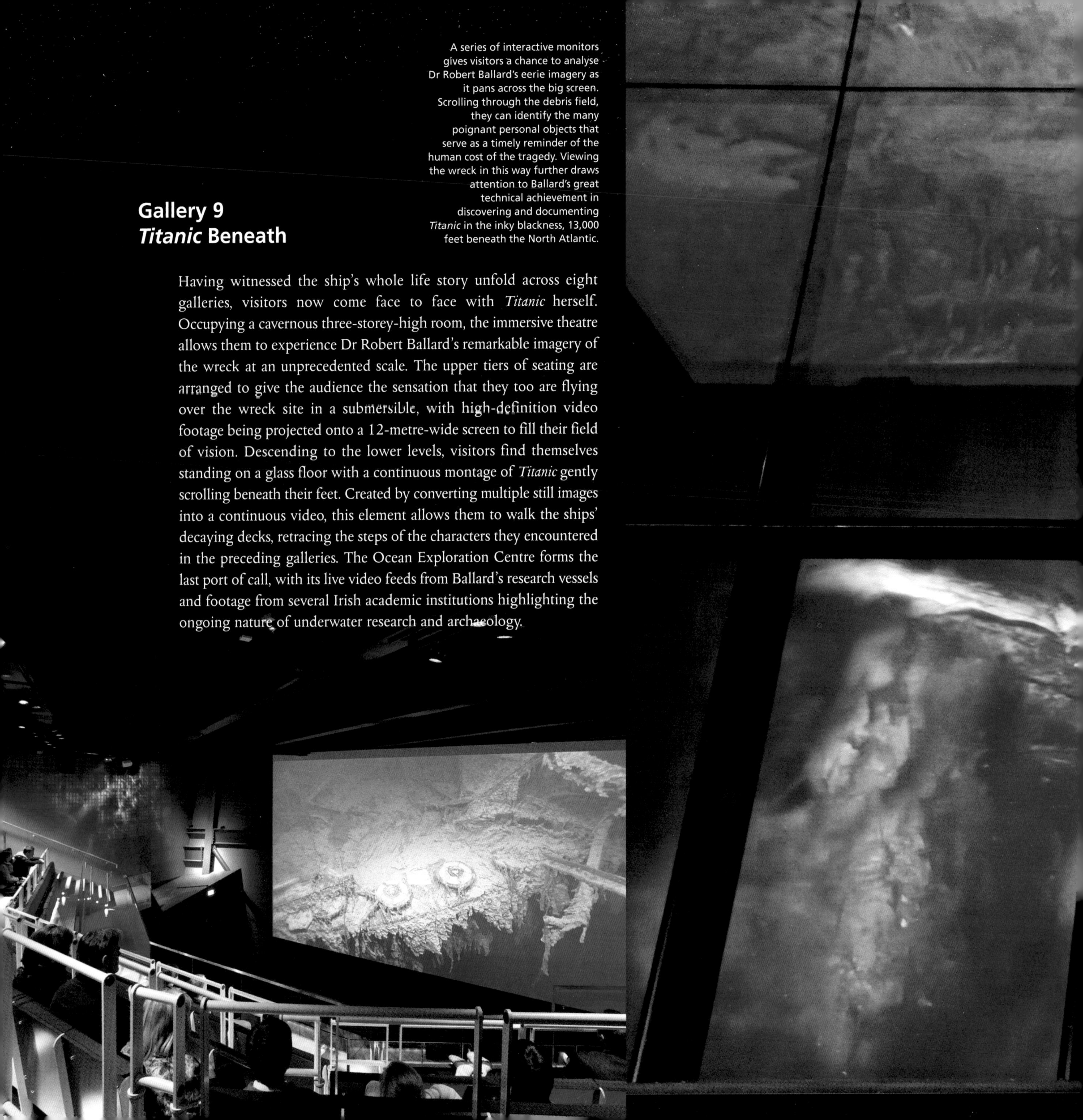

Gallery 9
Titanic Beneath

A series of interactive monitors gives visitors a chance to analyse Dr Robert Ballard's eerie imagery as it pans across the big screen. Scrolling through the debris field, they can identify the many poignant personal objects that serve as a timely reminder of the human cost of the tragedy. Viewing the wreck in this way further draws attention to Ballard's great technical achievement in discovering and documenting *Titanic* in the inky blackness, 13,000 feet beneath the North Atlantic.

Having witnessed the ship's whole life story unfold across eight galleries, visitors now come face to face with *Titanic* herself. Occupying a cavernous three-storey-high room, the immersive theatre allows them to experience Dr Robert Ballard's remarkable imagery of the wreck at an unprecedented scale. The upper tiers of seating are arranged to give the audience the sensation that they too are flying over the wreck site in a submersible, with high-definition video footage being projected onto a 12-metre-wide screen to fill their field of vision. Descending to the lower levels, visitors find themselves standing on a glass floor with a continuous montage of *Titanic* gently scrolling beneath their feet. Created by converting multiple still images into a continuous video, this element allows them to walk the ships' decaying decks, retracing the steps of the characters they encountered in the preceding galleries. The Ocean Exploration Centre forms the last port of call, with its live video feeds from Ballard's research vessels and footage from several Irish academic institutions highlighting the ongoing nature of underwater research and archaeology.

S
morning
sound of the ship yard
From the
N

A living landmark

Titanic Belfast was conceived from the outset as the cultural lynchpin of the Titanic Quarter. It was to be a place where the city's residents anc guests could freely mingle, rather than being reserved solely for the tourist trade. CivicArts hac been careful to place this iconic building at the heart of Harcourt's proposed Lagan Village development, furnishing it with generous public spaces and stunning vistas to form a natural focal point. This would be the town square for the local neighbourhood of offices, hotels and apartment blocks, where workers would come to sit and chat at lunchtime, and friends and familie could congregate of an evening.

As a monument to Belfast's industries, the building's exterio had to inspire, but its interior also had to deliver on that outwarc promise. Though its form was inspired by the hulls and gantrie from a world of hard work, the Great Atrium was envisaged a a relaxed 'living room for the city', whose doors would alway be open to the public without charge. Extending an oper invitation to Belfast's citizens, the quality and generosity of thes spaces enriches the island's public realm, as their storytellin qualities stretch out across every surface on a dramatic scale With its café, restaurant and shop, the building's public grounc plane remains ever lively, while, high above, the banqueting hal and its suite of private function rooms extend the hours o operation long into the night. Titanic Belfast was to be nc museum piece across whose threshold only ticket-holders coulc stroll. This was to be a living landmark for a modern Belfast.

The dark, industrial finishes of the Great Atrium take on a warmer hue when lit by artificial light at night. Rising five-storeys high and filled with jutting planes of timber and steel, it forms a theatrical lobby for evening functions in the banqueting suite.

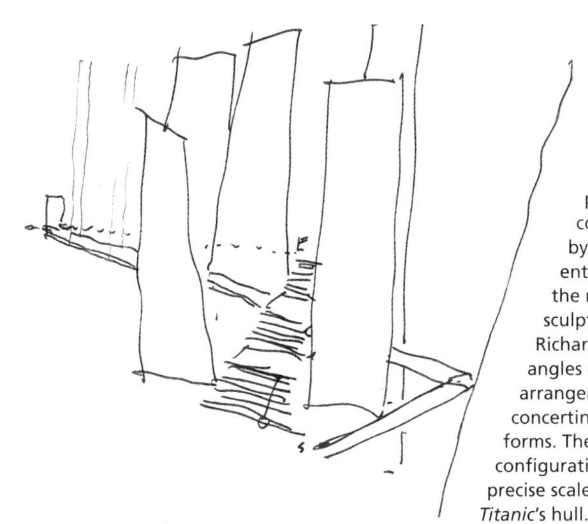
This early sketch by Eric Kuhne shows the jostling character of the plates as first conceived, inspired by both Event's entrance studies and the modern steel sculptures of artist Richard Serra. The angles of this loose arrangement gave way to concertinaed, folded forms. Their final configuration comprised precise scale sections of *Titanic*'s hull.

A grand entrance

The moment when guests first step inside Titanic Belfast had to be special. The beating heart of the building, the Great Atrium would be where the journey back to Belfast's past began, so the design team took care to make it a worthy prologue. CivicArts's original concept design embodied their narrative approach to architecture and interiors, with their layering of stories embedded in the fabric of the building. An analogy of the workspace beneath the Arrol Gantry, the tall, narrow proportions of the atrium became the void between the hulls of *Olympic* and *Titanic* as they neared completion. The galleries were to be entered on elevated walkways, like boarding-ramps, pushing past long plates of steel that hung over a wall of warm timber slats. The long lines of the black-painted escalators recalled the labyrinth of gangways that zigzagged up through the gantry, while everywhere the use of timber suggested both ships' decks and timber scaffolds. The wooden 'cribbage' that had supported the ship's frames in construction was translated into a lattice of louvres across the tall glazed 'fingers', filtering the late-afternoon sun as it pierced the deliberate, dark intensity of the space.

The informal layering of the early concept interiors contained echoes of the raw materials that were once stored on the exact site of the building. Stacked in plating racks, the oversized rolled plates arrived from the foundries by sea and were left in the open air until required. The platers would select a suitable plate from the rack, then take it to the platers' sheds, where it would be trimmed to size and punched with rivet holes.

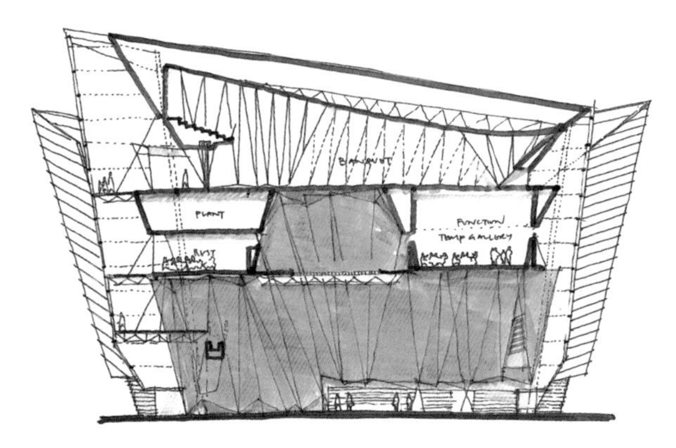

In the concept design, the atrium's soaring height allowed for instructive illustrations of scale. High above guests' heads hung a model of *Titanic*, suspended beneath a twinkling sky of fibre-optic constellations that transformed the ceiling into the northern skies as they were on that fateful night of 14th/15th April 1912. The model was scaled so that distance between it and the atrium floor was the same as the depth to which *Titanic* sank. The atrium's centrepiece was a stone compass rose, whose gleaming brass rhumb lines radiated out into the surrounding plaza, connecting it to its historic context.

Fractured hull

Having begun as vertical echoes of the external cladding's crystal shards, the hanging array of steel plates slowly evolved to become full-scale reproductions of *Titanic*'s hull plating. Complete with pre-drilled holes for rivets and sidelights, they took full advantage of the five-storey-high space, offering guests a tangible sense of *Titanic*'s scale as they entered the atrium to begin their journey. The dizzying intensity of jutting angles, tiered observation platforms and interlacing escalators all combined to form a powerful analogy – not only of the gantries and cranes, but also of the cathedral-like cavern of the great ship's engine room. The tactile palette of steel, wood, glass and stone combined the solidity of Edwardian craftsmanship with twenty-first-century computer-aided design. An exemplary essay in narrative architecture, the Great Atrium's concept design was an evocative tribute to the industry of Belfast's shipbuilders and demonstrated the potential of this monumental space to inspire all who crossed its threshold.

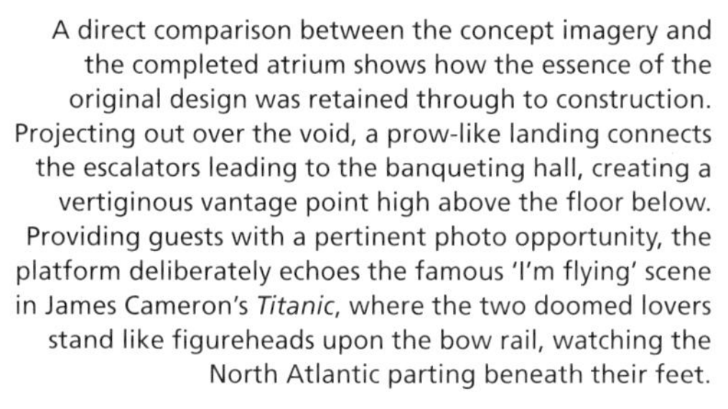

A direct comparison between the concept imagery and the completed atrium shows how the essence of the original design was retained through to construction. Projecting out over the void, a prow-like landing connects the escalators leading to the banqueting hall, creating a vertiginous vantage point high above the floor below. Providing guests with a pertinent photo opportunity, the platform deliberately echoes the famous 'I'm flying' scene in James Cameron's *Titanic*, where the two doomed lovers stand like figureheads upon the bow rail, watching the North Atlantic parting beneath their feet.

To create an immersive experience from the point of entry, Kay Elliott's early concept had visitors approach the galleries via staggered ramps, with *Titanic*'s black hull being unexpectedly revealed behind a cloaking screen of rusted plating as they turned the corner.

The atrium evolves

With the concept phase complete, the design development and delivery of Titanic Belfast's interiors was assigned to Torquay-based practice Kay Elliott. Their role as overall design consultants for the interior made them a unifying link between the many different firms who would be required during the fit-out. With their extensive experience of developing popular visitor attractions, from Paignton Zoo to the London Eye, Kay Elliott could offer a wide range of expertise. They conducted their own research into the history of both Belfast and *Titanic* before making their proposals.

Like CivicArts, they saw the atrium as a major opportunity for conveying the immense scale of the *Olympic*-class liners and offered several alternatives for the wayfinding, graphics, feature wall and entrance. The concept of entering the gallery along similar stepped ramps to those used to ascend the Arrol Gantry was explored, but these and many other ideas were hamstrung by the advanced stage of the build. With the concrete poured and steelwork on order, all proposals had to work within the existing structure, which was growing by the day. One of the most significant changes from the concept phase was the altering of the alignment of the feature wall's steel plates from vertical to horizontal, creating a closer analogy of *Titanic*'s hull under construction. Visitors would now enter through the ship's side, as though the plates had been peeled back to reveal its inner workings.

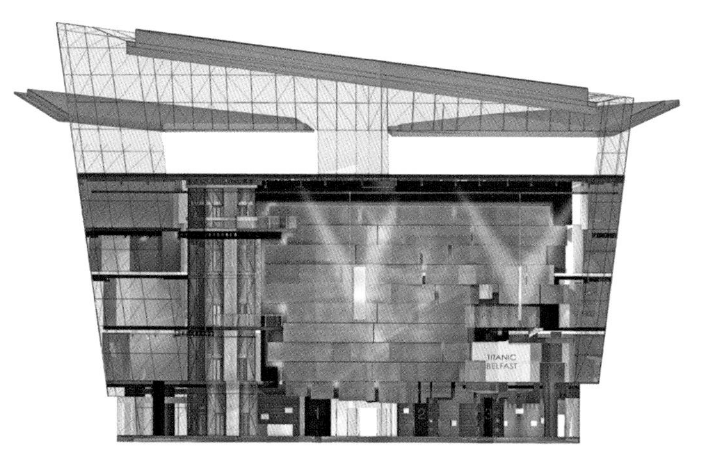

The tall proportions of the Great Atrium allowed the wall's abstract arrangement of plates to be the same height as the distance from the turn of *Titanic*'s bilge keel to the point on C-deck where her white paint began. Facing it is the graphic 'Ship Wall', created by Tandem Design, recording the names and hull numbers of the first 401 vessels built by Harland & Wolff, with *Titanic* and *Olympic* featuring most prominently.

Titanic-scale cladding

It was the world's largest ship when launched, and *Titanic*'s individual components were similarly colossal in size. The inch-thick steel plates that formed her sides measured an average of 6 feet tall by 30 feet long. The final design for the east feature wall emphasised the horizontal alignment of these overlapping strakes of steel, with acid-treated steel panels sized to match the original fabric of the ship. Despite the wall's shift from vertical to horizontal, a link to the building's external appearance was maintained through its architectural treatment. With the help of Spanwall and Todd Architects, the Kay Elliott concept was converted into a lightweight steel cladding system, so that real plate metal could be used instead of a simulated paint finish. The partially rusted patina was chosen to suggest work in progress, as the raw materials, exposed to the Belfast weather in the open yards, were slowly transformed into luxury liners.

Booths beneath the hull

The hull analogy continued beneath the feature wall, so that the narrative wrapped around the visitor's ground-floor point of entry. The staggered steel ceiling panels exaggerated the overlapping clencher-built construction of *Titanic*'s flat-bottomed hull, giving a sense of the ship's immense weight bearing down upon its keel blocks during construction. The stacked piles of heavy timbers upon which the keel was laid were reinterpreted as blackened ticket booths, with circular porthole-style windows.

These early studies for the ticket booths employed a more open structure, derived from taller stacks of keel blocks near Titanic's bows. The final design resembled the tightly packed stepped pyramids of keel blocks that supported the hull, that extended down the slipway like wooden vertebrae..

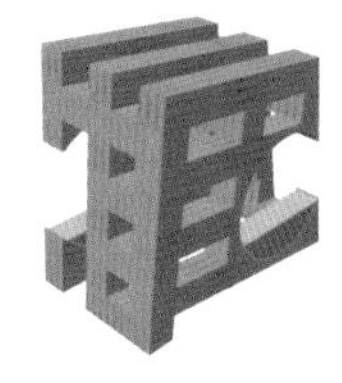

Stories on the walls

With one wall of the atrium clad in steel, there remained many large surfaces with the potential for conveying stories of the shipyards. The design team explored several different avenues that would express the scale, skill and labour that this site once witnessed. The final scheme was devised by Belfast-based consultants Tandem Design, who created a system of clean-cut graphics that could add a layer of detail to the vast expanses of wall. At basement level, technical drawings of *Titanic*'s components were reproduced at full size so that visitors could stand next to the ghostly outlines of the anchors, boilers and propeller bosses that dwarfed the men who made them. The generously sized entrance to the basement toilets still only manages to occupy a quarter of one immense engine casting. The 'Ship Wall', which rises above the Galley Café, records the names of the first 401 vessels constructed by Harland & Wolff, deliberately arranged with the graphic density of an Edwardian wooden letterpress. Largest of all are the characters who populate the landings, the tallest of whom is the haughty first-class wine waiter who watches guests approach the banqueting hall along the escalators.

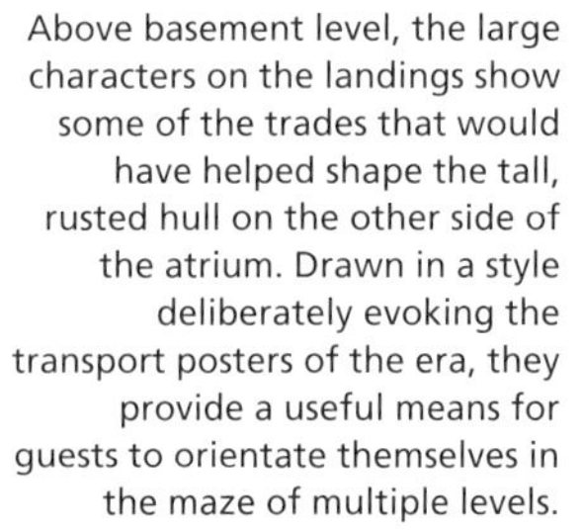

Above basement level, the large characters on the landings show some of the trades that would have helped shape the tall, rusted hull on the other side of the atrium. Drawn in a style deliberately evoking the transport posters of the era, they provide a useful means for guests to orientate themselves in the maze of multiple levels.

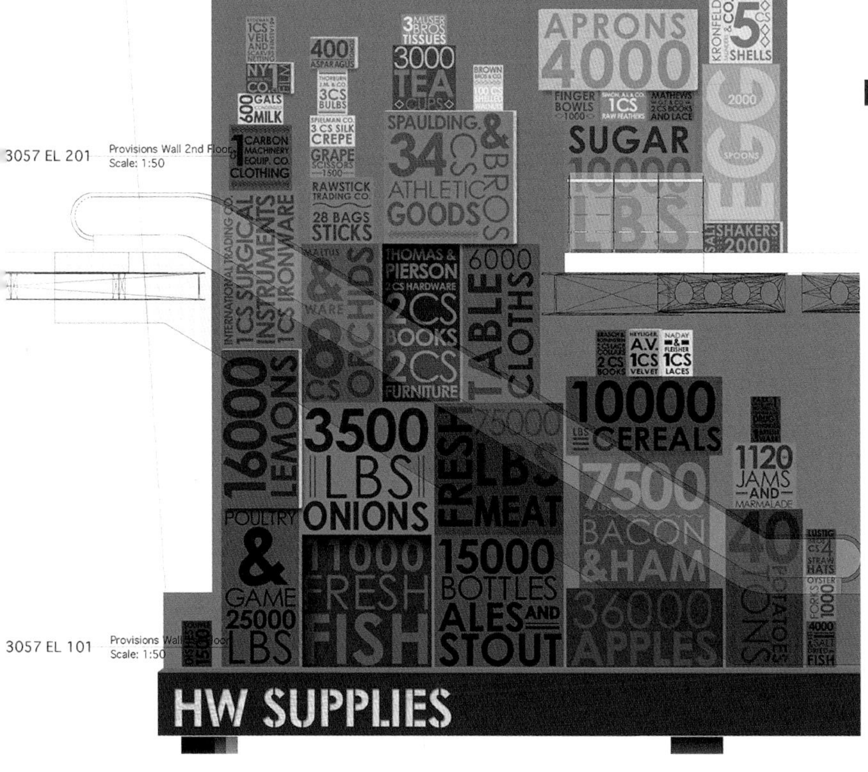

Finding your way

As a deliberate counterpoint to the literal renderings of full-sized hull sections, keel blocks and technical drawings, Kay Elliott explored more indirect means of conveying the scale at which all activities surrounding *Titanic* had to operate. An early proposal was for a 'Provisions Wall', with stylised depictions of stores being stacked on the quayside ready to be swung aboard the ship for her maiden voyage. The intention was for these bold facts and figures to be printed on wooden panels of varying thicknesses to give texture to the vast wall spaces. They drew attention to the statistics of luxury transatlantic travel by recording the 29,000 pieces of glassware, 36,000 apples and no fewer than 8,000 cigars that White Star deemed essential for passenger comfort. Though later superseded by Tandem's designs, the concept provided the genesis for the atrium's distinctive wayfinders, which assume the form of staggered stacks of polished hardwood boxes whose labels direct visitors around the building.

O city of sound and motion!
O city of endless stir!
From the dawn of a misty morning,
To the fall of the evening air;
From the night of the moving shadows,
To the sound of the shipyard horn;
We hail thee Queen of the Northland,
We who are Belfast born.

'Men of Belfast', from *Songs from the Shipyards*, 1924
Thomas Carnduff (1896–1956)

The Belfast poet Thomas Carnduff, pictured in 1922 when he was working as a gas inspector. Often described as 'the shipyards' playwright', Carnduff spent his whole life working in and around the Belfast shipyards, where he had first served as a catch-boy in a riveting squad, aged just 14. As a playwright, poet and essayist, he found inspiration in the city's industrial landscape and its people, as well as in his wartime experiences with the Royal Engineers.

The compass rose

A great room needs a great centrepiece, and the debate about what to place at the heart of Titanic Belfast continued until late into 2011, when the flooring began to be laid. With the design of the surrounding plaza confirmed as a map of the northern hemisphere, tracing *Titanic*'s maiden voyage, it was decided to continue the theme of navigation and return to CivicArts's original concept of an imposing compass rose. Composed of contrasting stone pavers and inlaid with stainless steel, the facets of the revised design deliberately referenced the jagged, three-dimensional aesthetic of the exterior aluminium panels. With its points aligned to the map's meridians, the circumference of the compass was inscribed with the stirring first stanza of 'Men of Belfast', penned by local poet and plater's assistant Thomas Carnduff. A poetic epitaph to men who laboured on Queen's Island, the radiating compass rose reminds visitors that the ships that were built here went on to sail around the globe.

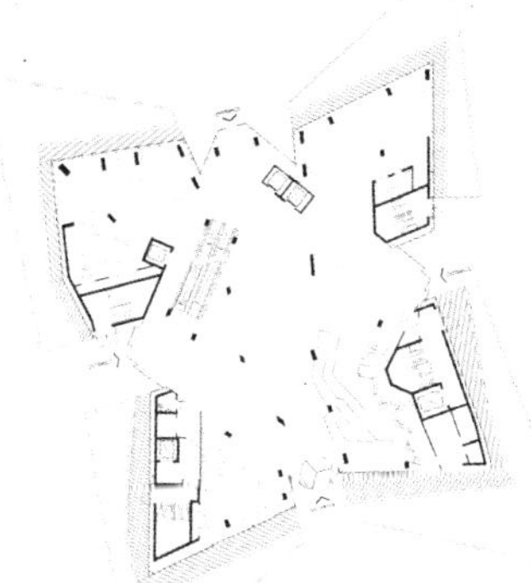

Atrium ambience

Recent years have seen the rise of museums and galleries as popular public venues, with the British Museum's accessible Great Court and the Tate Modern's bookshop and restaurant becoming fashionable meeting places. Titanic Belfast was likewise envisaged as a social hub whose atrium activities would function in parallel with its main visitor attraction. The task of creating inviting retail and dining areas was assigned to the Irish firm of O'Donnell O'Neill Design Associates, who worked with Marcon Fit-Out to deliver convincing extensions of the wider atrium themes. The pristine white tiling and wooden tables of Bistro 401 have a clean Edwardian efficiency about them, and its menu serves to showcase some of Northern Ireland's finest produce beneath a glass ceiling depicting the internal decoration of the White Star liners. The Galley café adopts a more informal, industrial canteen aesthetic in which to serve its snacks and full barista range.

A mecca for the *Titanic* enthusiast, or for those just wishing to buy a unique souvenir, the Titanic Store is lined with riveted metal panels as if the merchandise was being transported in *Titanic*'s hold. Delicate gifts and luxury objects are imaginatively displayed in open, oversized travelling trunks. Busy, bustling and accessible to all, the amenities of the Great Atrium make it a welcoming place to meet all year round.

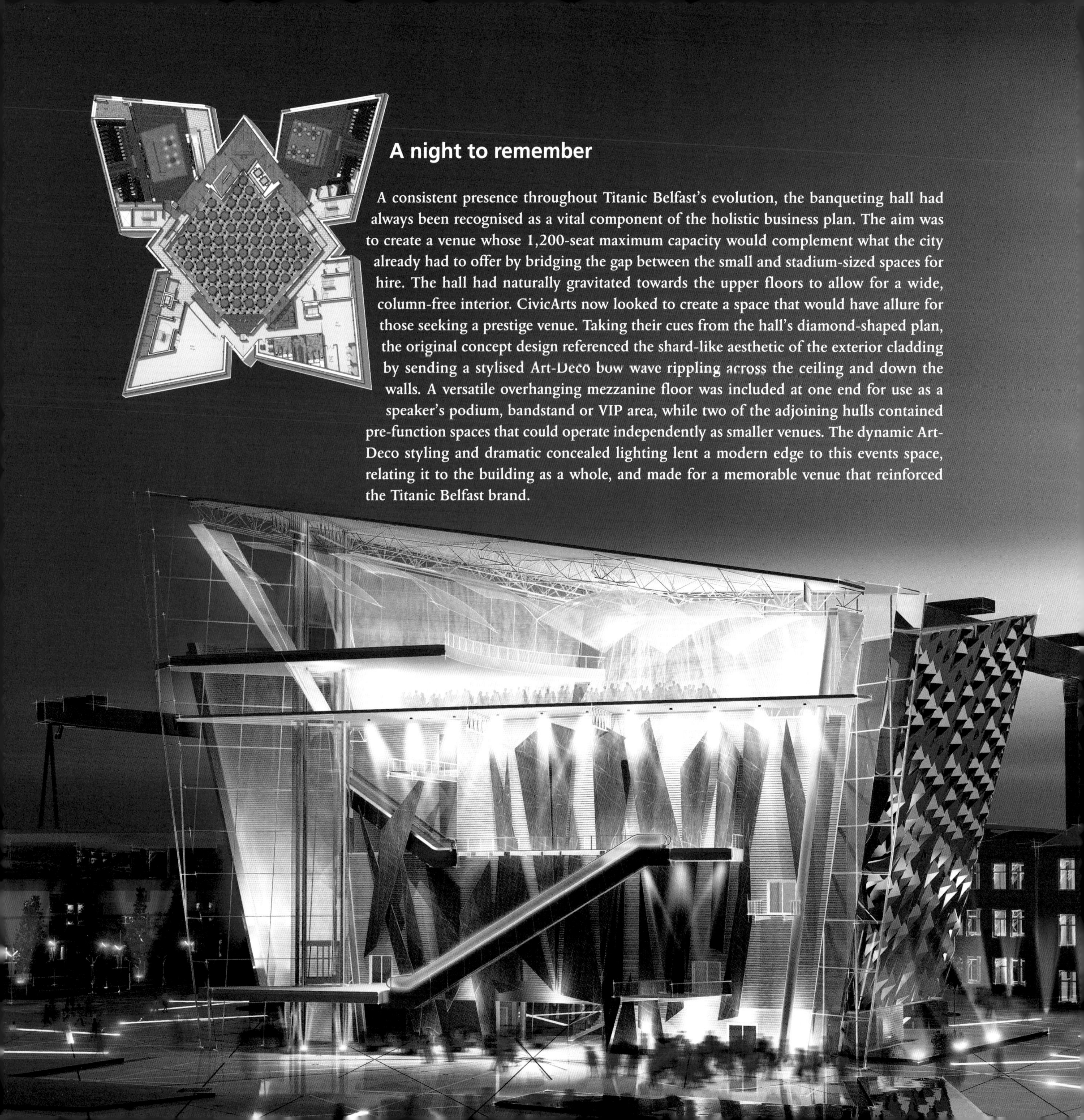

A night to remember

A consistent presence throughout Titanic Belfast's evolution, the banqueting hall had always been recognised as a vital component of the holistic business plan. The aim was to create a venue whose 1,200-seat maximum capacity would complement what the city already had to offer by bridging the gap between the small and stadium-sized spaces for hire. The hall had naturally gravitated towards the upper floors to allow for a wide, column-free interior. CivicArts now looked to create a space that would have allure for those seeking a prestige venue. Taking their cues from the hall's diamond-shaped plan, the original concept design referenced the shard-like aesthetic of the exterior cladding by sending a stylised Art-Deco bow wave rippling across the ceiling and down the walls. A versatile overhanging mezzanine floor was included at one end for use as a speaker's podium, bandstand or VIP area, while two of the adjoining hulls contained pre-function spaces that could operate independently as smaller venues. The dynamic Art-Deco styling and dramatic concealed lighting lent a modern edge to this events space, relating it to the building as a whole, and made for a memorable venue that reinforced the Titanic Belfast brand.

Dubbed 'The Board Room', the second pre-function space design embodied the craftsmanship of the inter-war luxury liners. The frosted-glass room partition displayed a pictorial map of the North Atlantic, while the painted *trompe l'oeil* ceiling portrayed a gallery of Queen's Island's luminaries gathered along a ship's rail.

The first pre-function-space concept design evoked the Edwardian panelled interiors of luxury cabins or gentlemen's clubs, with builder's ship models arranged in deep niches around leather armchairs. Above them floated a glowing polar azimuthally equidistant map of the world, marked with the major shipping routes.

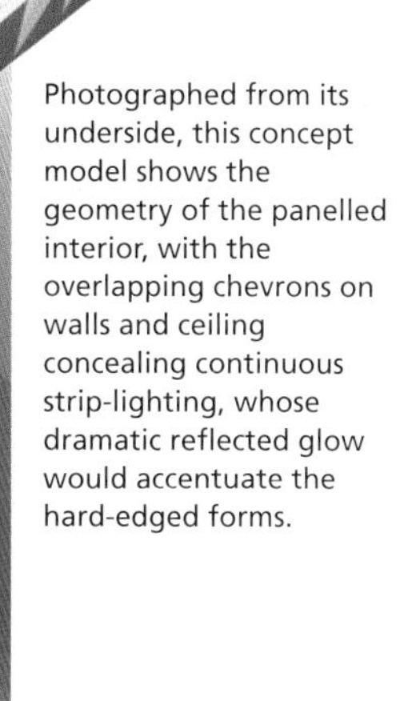

Photographed from its underside, this concept model shows the geometry of the panelled interior, with the overlapping chevrons on walls and ceiling concealing continuous strip-lighting, whose dramatic reflected glow would accentuate the hard-edged forms.

Making room for a legend

It was a central element to the *Titanic* legend that caused the design of the banqueting hall to dramatically change direction. Featured in nearly every cinematic account of the disaster, the ornate Grand Staircase acted as a three-dimensional theatrical backdrop across which the themes of Edwardian hubris and class division could be explored. The final dream sequence of James Cameron's *Titanic* sees the camera sweep up the stair as two lovers from opposite ends of the social spectrum are reunited beneath the delicate tracery of its glass-domed ceiling. Recognising the power of this popular image, Pat Doherty and the Harcourt board had long harboured a wish for the staircase to be recreated within this, the world's premier *Titanic*-themed attraction. Therefore, the options for its inclusion were investigated. The scale of this set piece presented serious space issues and, as options for its inclusion were explored, it became clear that it could not be worked into the galleries, one of which already boasted a virtual facsimile of the stair in the 'Cave'. If it was to be a functioning staircase, not a static exhibit, the only place this *Titanic* icon could find a home was in the lofty banqueting hall.

Like her sister *Titanic*, *Olympic* had two grand staircases, each spanning decks A to F and reserved for the exclusive use of first-class passengers. Titanic Belfast's staircase was to be based upon the surviving photographs of *Olympic*'s forward stair, recreating its elaborate A Deck landing, complete with carved clock panel and bronze cherub candelabrum, lit from above by a curving glass dome.

Titanic's wooden fittings are long gone, but the ornately carved first-class-lounge decorations of her sister ship were auctioned off when the *Olympic* was scrapped in 1937. They were re-used to create the Olympic Suite in the White Swan Hotel in Alnwick, Northumberland, which provides a tangible sense of the *Olympic*-class liners' opulence. Kay Elliott's Edwardian-inspired scheme evolved over several permutations of classically derived columns and mouldings, many of them designed to conceal essential services such as power and ventilation.

With overall responsibility for the interiors, Kay Elliott were set the challenge both of recreating the Grand Staircase in all its Edwardian glory and of integrating it within the banqueting hall. Clearly, the insertion of such a large mass of period detailing would not sit comfortably with the Art Deco aesthetics of the original CivicArts concept and so an entirely new scheme of decoration had to be devised. Rather than creating a direct pastiche of *Titanic*'s eclectic first-class décor, Kay Elliott sought to celebrate the spirit of the ship's luxurious fit-out, using a palette of modern materials. Selecting period details that could be adapted to this expansive modern volume, they aimed to create a suite of function spaces that combined the grandeur of *Titanic*'s staterooms with the easy comfort of a gentlemen's club.

All of the staircase's 11 elaborate wrought-iron-style panels were different shapes and sizes. BMC experimented with traditional techniques, using a gas forge and vintage power hammer to fabricate the central oval elements. Combining forged and cast components, these were then painted black before being embellished with real gold leaf.

Local skills

Though *Titanic*'s Grand Staircase is no more, surviving fragments of *Olympic*'s elaborately carved interiors provide a hint of her sister's Edwardian opulence. After making a detailed study of the archive photographs, fragments and decks plans, Kay Elliott began to design a staircase that would retain the spirit of the original while conforming to the stringent needs of modern health and safety legislation. Constrained by the structural steelwork and the configuration of the hall, it was not possible to produce a replica exact in every detail, but the careful draughtsmanship of conservation architect, Peter Bancroft, clearly displayed a richness that honoured the original.

The skills to turn these plans into reality were found just 40 miles down the road from Belfast in Bellaghy, where Oldtown Joinery had their workshops, next door to BMC Engineering. Beginning with a substantial pine and plywood carcass, Oldtown's team of craftsmen began six months of patient work to create the banqueting hall's showpiece staircase. The stair's complex curves called for a host of different techniques, from steaming and laminating to bespoke router-cut mouldings. Slowly, panel by panel, the ghost of the Grand Staircase was resurrected.

Though aided by modern power tools, the team still had to do a great deal of work by hand. Working by eye, as well as from plan, master craftsmen Sean Diamond and Peter Kearns kept a tight control of the staircase's sweeping curves to ensure the multiple components would blend smoothly together. The substantial banisters were formed from box-sections of plywood, which were slowly clad and profiled with successive laminations of moulded American red oak.

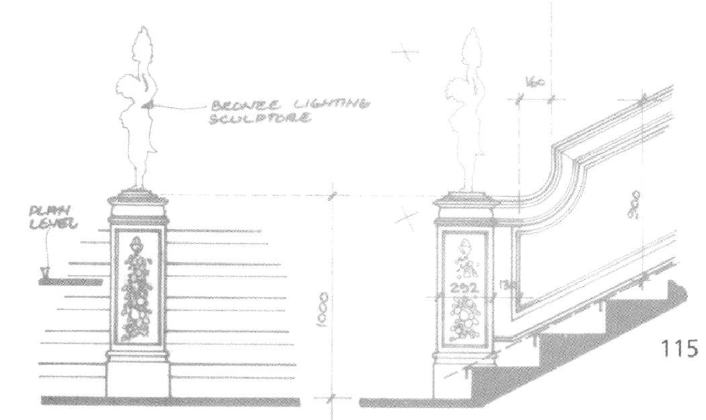

The focal point of the composition, the central clock with its figurative panelled surround, is a replica of the surviving timepiece from *Olympic*'s Grand Staircase, which had similar features to *Titanic*'s. Carved by the artist Charles Wilson to represent 'Honour and Glory crowning Time', this original fixture is now preserved in Southampton's SeaCity Museum. Paragon used a clay model to make a plaster mould from which a resin cast could be taken and then woodgrained to blend with Oldtown's joinery.

Finishing touches

The arrival of the staircase onsite in August 2011 was as dramatic as the films that made it famous. Even when divided into sub-assemblies, the massive timber elements were too large to ascend to the fifth floor by lift. Access doors on the upper reaches of the mezzanine were opened and the sections hoisted up by crane. Once set down on the building's summit, it took more than 20 men to carry the sections down a temporary stair of scaffolding and bring them to their final destination. Oldtown Joinery then set up shop in the banqueting hall and began to reassemble this timber jigsaw puzzle, applying the varnish, stain and polish that would make the red oak glow. Finishing touches included installing the stairs' brass nosing and handrails and wiring in the candelabrum, held aloft by its bronze-painted cherub. Both the impish lamp and ornate clock surround were the work of craftsmen from Paragon Creative, who were also the principal set-makers for the galleries below.

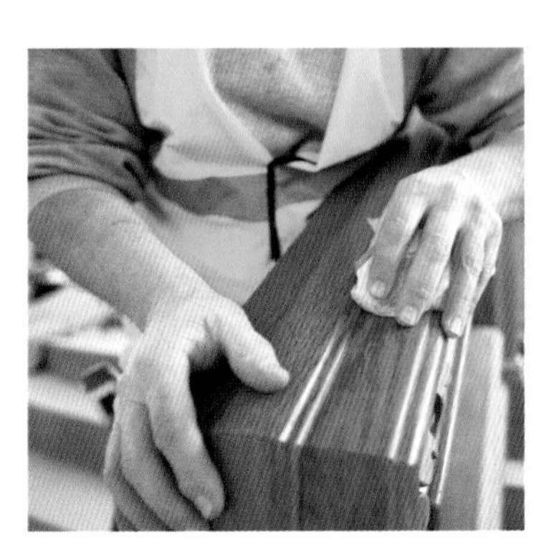

A venue like no other

With the Grand Staircase as its commanding centrepiece, Belfast's newest banqueting hall now possessed a natural sense of theatre. The ring of walkways and balconies wrapped around the hall's perimeter allowed speakers to emerge from the wings and dramatically descend the stairs to address the waiting audience. The craftsmanship invested in that staircase was not the only modern echo of *Titanic*'s original fit-out in the hall's design. Built largely of metal like a ship's framed hull, the upper storeys of Titanic Belfast had likewise to be lined and insulated to create the luxurious accommodation of a prestige venue. The hall's deeply coffered ceiling, with its backlit moulded surrounds, was a two-way acoustic solution – it would shield local residents from the sound of late night revelries, while insulating the assembled guests from the sound of rain on the zinc-clad roof above. With its bespoke interior and unique position on Queen's Island, this lofty, light-filled space was now a venue like no other.

Reshaping the shipyards

However compelling the final form and content of Titanic Belfast may be, it is its context that ultimately anchors it in the collective imagination. It was Queen's Island's status as the birthplace of *Titanic* that set the Signature Project in motion, for it presented a unique site carrying an unparalleled seal of authenticity.

It was upon these very slipways that the skilled workers of Harland & Wolff laboured for two years and two months to complete the hull of the largest ship the world had ever seen. The decision to preserve the open 'hallowed ground' where *Titanic*'s hull once rested proved a key point in the project's evolution, but the work did not end with simply locating the building at the slipways' head. Levelled to form a car park, then left to decay, the derelict slipways would need to be nurtured back to life if they were to be made accessible to the anticipated volume of visitors from around the world. Reinventing this former shipyard as the landscaped heart of the future Titanic Quarter called for an integrated design approach, combining ideas from several parties to produce a scheme that would do justice to the site's rich story. Not for the first time, Queen's Island was to be reshaped to meet the needs of the city it had helped make famous.

Graphically illustrating the ship's true dimensions, the paving of the former No.3 slip allows visitors to walk the length of *Titanic*'s boat deck like passengers on its maiden voyage. Within its outline stands one of the two concrete bow blocks, now preserved within a frame of toughened glass panels to form a memorial to all who lost their lives in connection with *Titanic*'s short existence.

Shipbuilders to the world

Forming an integral part of its Titanic Quarter masterplan, CivicArts's detailed concept design for a public plaza united the slipways and the Signature Project within a continuous narrative. Their intricate scheme recognised the historic global significance of Belfast's shipyards, for the hundreds of vessels built and launched from the banks of the River Lagan once formed an invisible chain around the earth, linking this trading port with countless others across the world. The footprint of the future Titanic Belfast lay at the heart of this international enterprise, occupying the former site of the plate racks and platers' sheds dividing the North and South Yards of Harland & Wolff. Taking the global theme of maritime navigation, the plaza derived its rich design from antique maps, as though an immense Admiralty chart had been rolled out across the island. The outlines of *Olympic* and *Titanic* were to be retraced upon the slipways, with their bows symbolically overlapping the plaza's rhumb lines as a reminder of their role within the history of transatlantic travel. Envisaged as an active social hub, the plaza was provided with café pavilions, whose tables would spill out in the summer months for patrons to enjoy the play of light across the project's gleaming aluminium cladding, magnified by the shallow reflecting pools beneath. All this combined to create a public meeting place that honoured Queen's Island's Victorian origins as the 'People's Park' of Belfast.

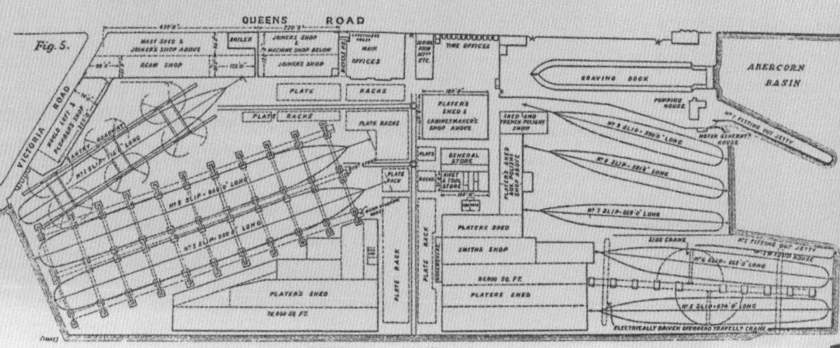

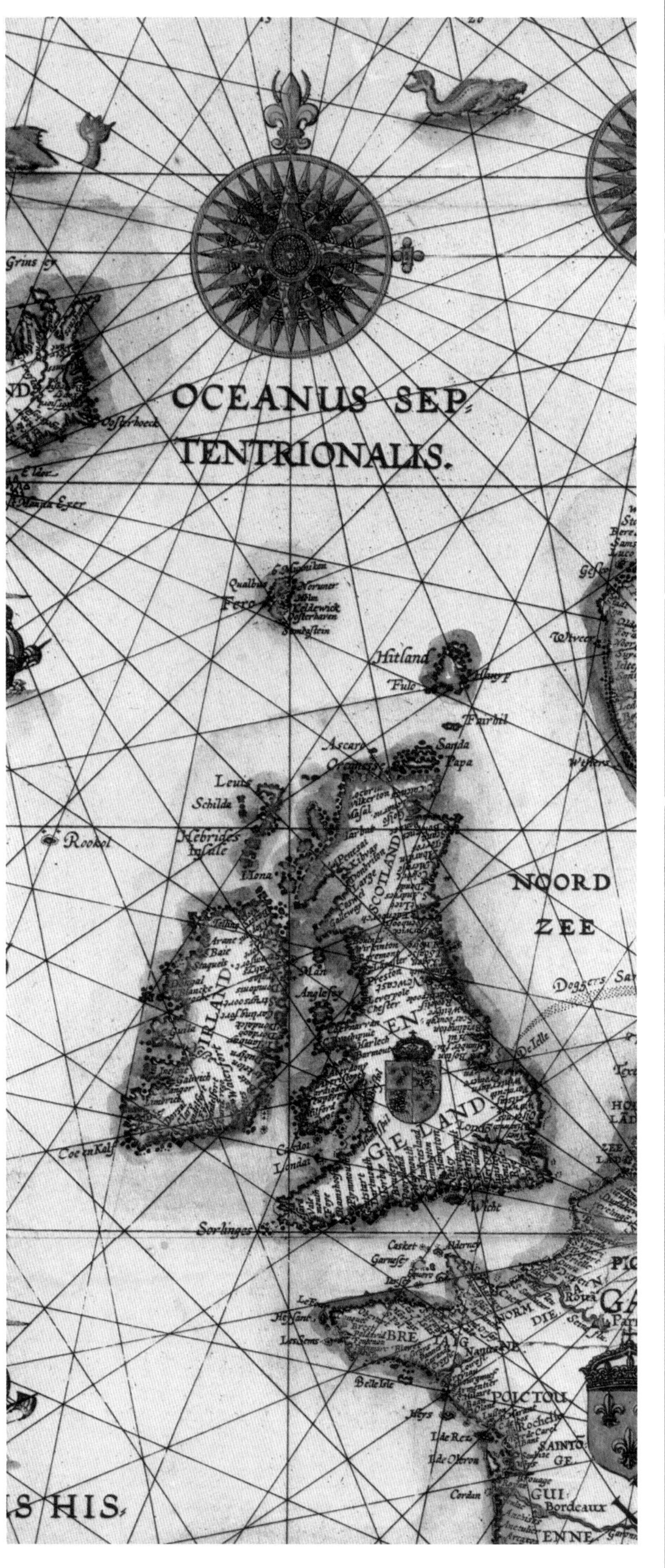

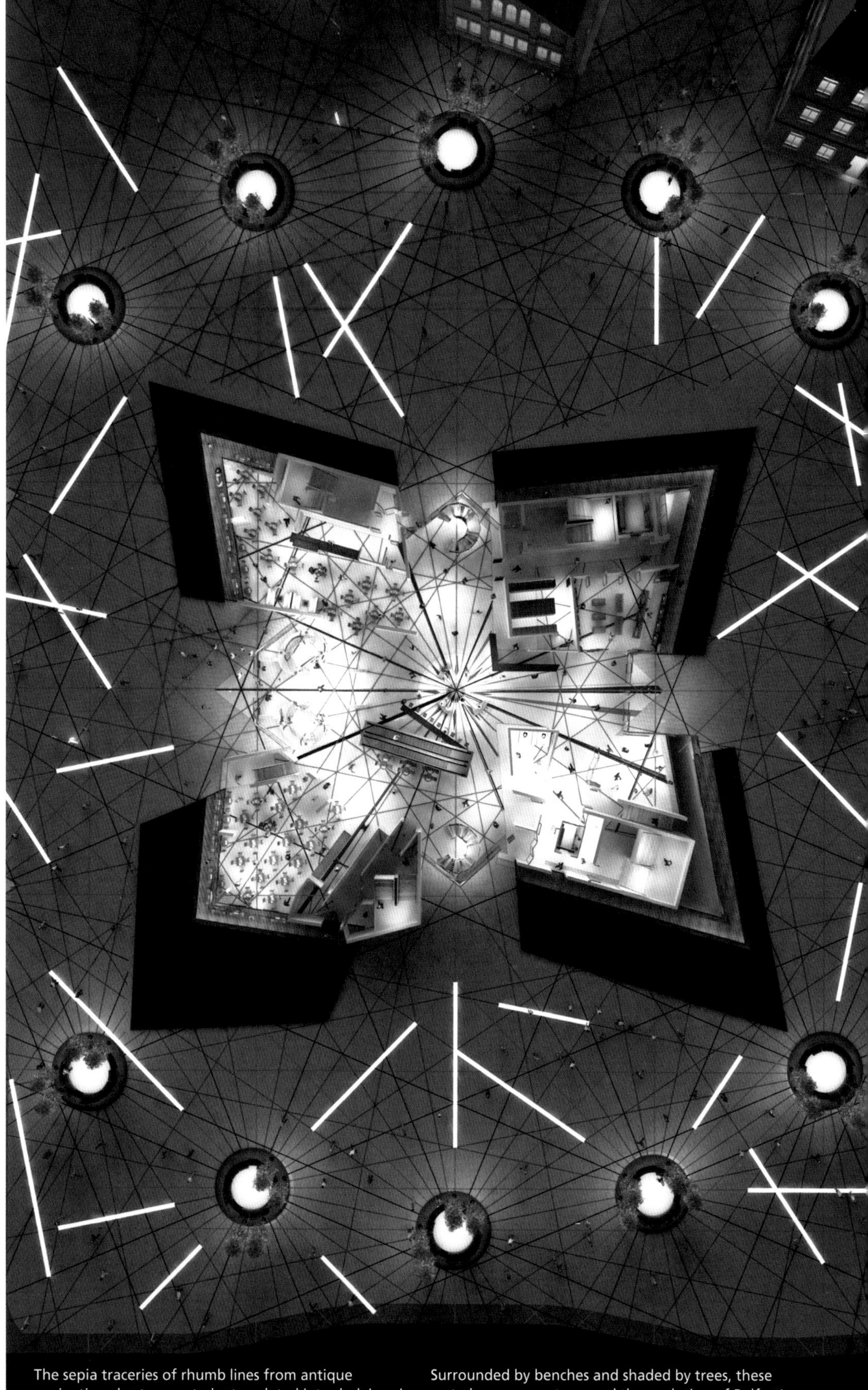

The sepia traceries of rhumb lines from antique navigation charts were to be translated into dark bands of brass or granite, emanating from the atrium's central compass rose. Passing through the outer walls, they spread across the surrounding plaza to intersect with a ring of circular brass plaques aligned with the 16 subdivisions of the four cardinal directions.

Surrounded by benches and shaded by trees, these cast plaques were to record the evolution of Belfast's port and harbour through raised facsimiles of historic maps. Sections of this web of navigational aids were replaced by underlit glass strips, creating dynamic 'light wands' to add an extra dimension to the building's nocturnal identity.

Inspired by the ornamental flowerbeds to be found in Belfast's lush Botanic Gardens, CivicArts's concept for the historic slipways laid out a gracious formal garden extending all the way to the water's edge. Reproduced at full size, the respective outlines of *Titanic*'s and *Olympic*'s saloon and shelter decks provided the templates for a sequence of flower-filled parterres and box-hedged garden rooms, connected by paths of granite flagstones. Clear areas of stone and timber landscaping were reserved for marquees to be erected, providing events space for markets, fairs and alfresco dining as required. Bordered by avenues of trees, the central line of the original Arrol Gantry's stanchions was recalled by the ranks of slender steel masts whose floodlights would allow the slipways to remain active after dark. This ambitious concept offered a gracious public amenity for Belfast, embedded within a tangible illustration of *Titanic*'s scale.

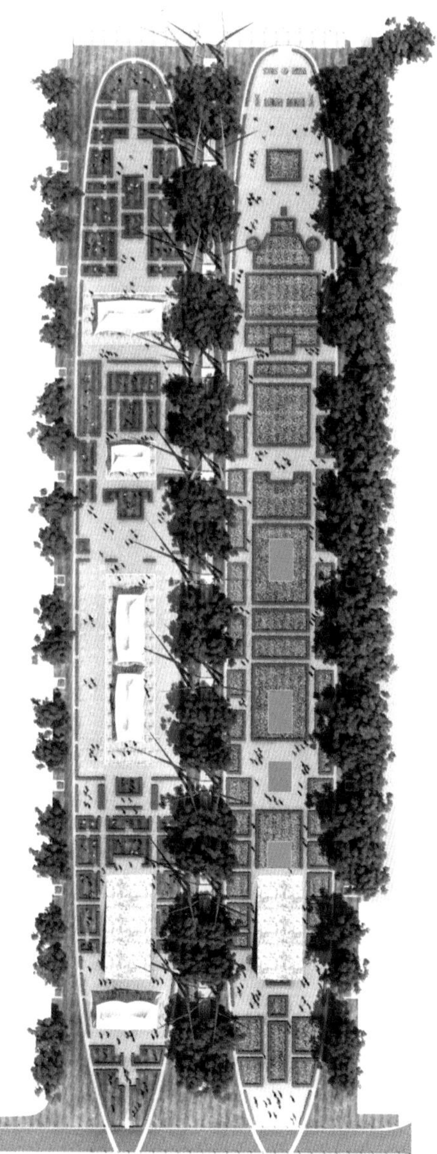

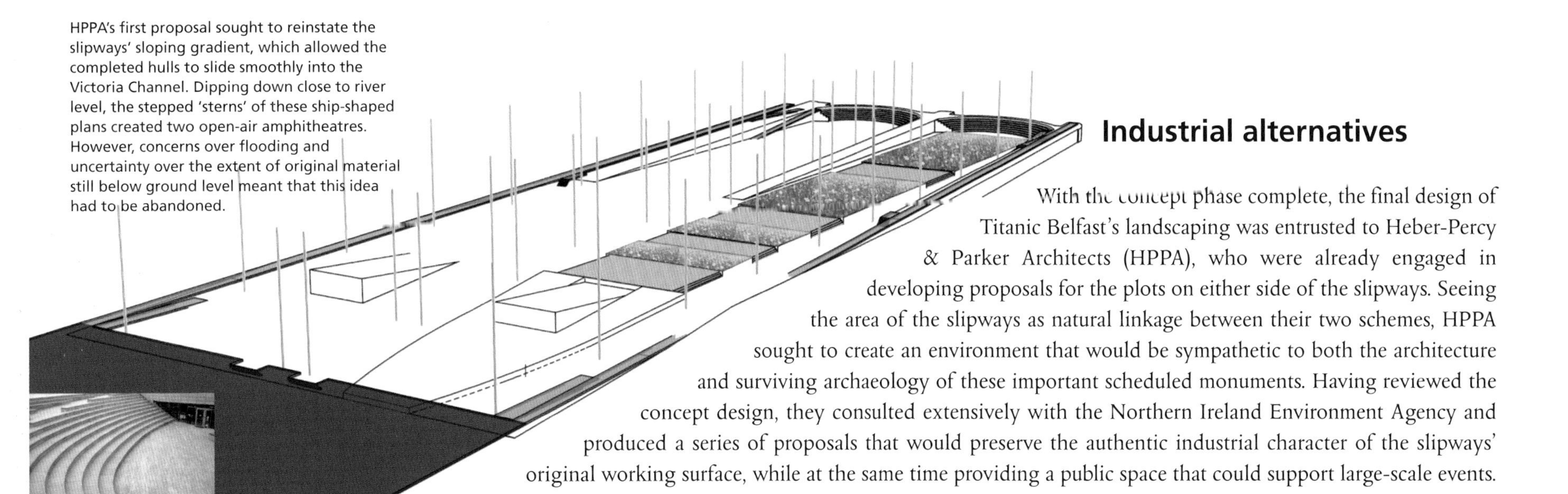

HPPA's first proposal sought to reinstate the slipways' sloping gradient, which allowed the completed hulls to slide smoothly into the Victoria Channel. Dipping down close to river level, the stepped 'sterns' of these ship-shaped plans created two open-air amphitheatres. However, concerns over flooding and uncertainty over the extent of original material still below ground level meant that this idea had to be abandoned.

Industrial alternatives

With the concept phase complete, the final design of Titanic Belfast's landscaping was entrusted to Heber-Percy & Parker Architects (HPPA), who were already engaged in developing proposals for the plots on either side of the slipways. Seeing the area of the slipways as natural linkage between their two schemes, HPPA sought to create an environment that would be sympathetic to both the architecture and surviving archaeology of these important scheduled monuments. Having reviewed the concept design, they consulted extensively with the Northern Ireland Environment Agency and produced a series of proposals that would preserve the authentic industrial character of the slipways' original working surface, while at the same time providing a public space that could support large-scale events.

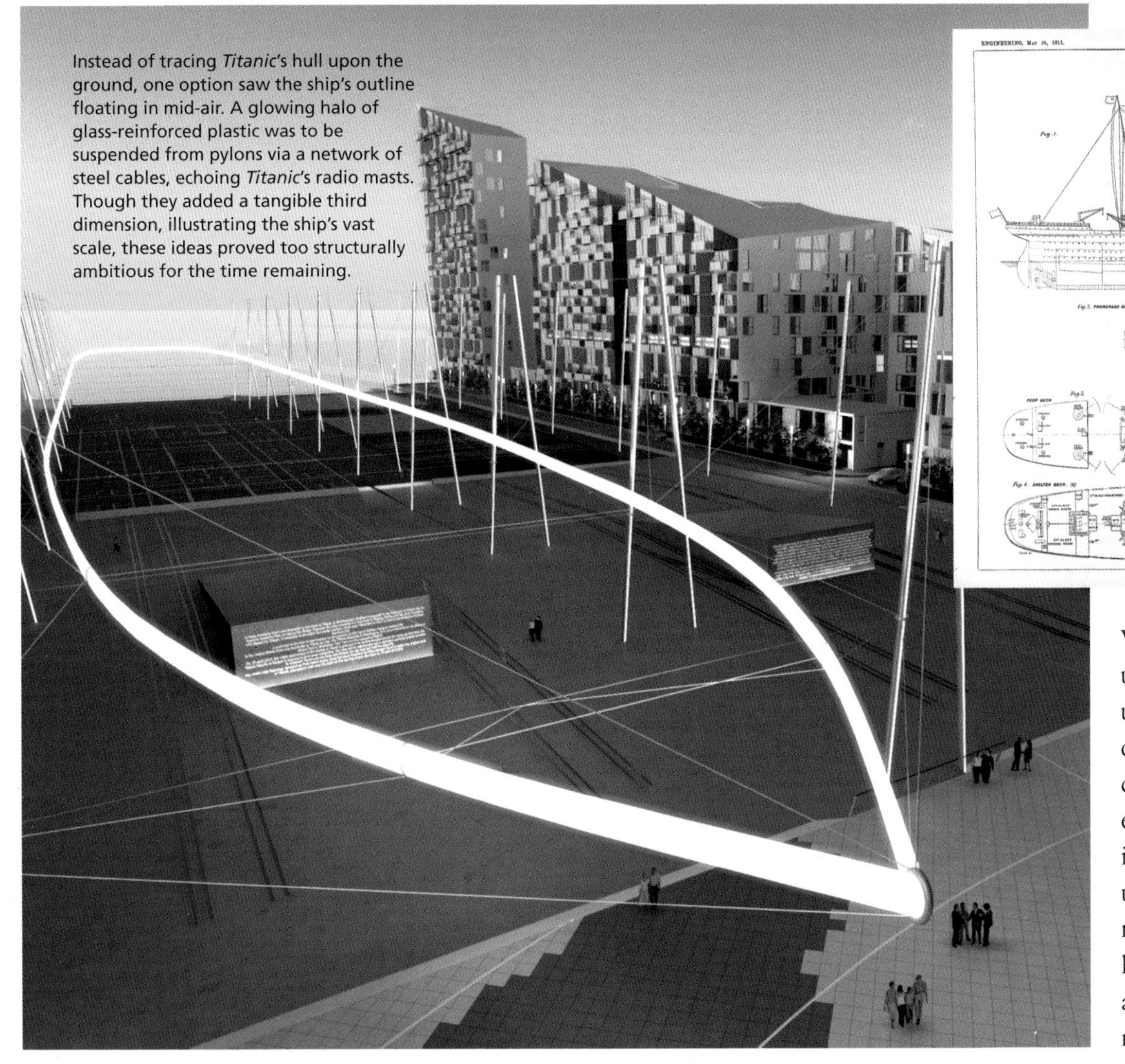

Instead of tracing *Titanic*'s hull upon the ground, one option saw the ship's outline floating in mid-air. A glowing halo of glass-reinforced plastic was to be suspended from pylons via a network of steel cables, echoing *Titanic*'s radio masts. Though they added a tangible third dimension, illustrating the ship's vast scale, these ideas proved too structurally ambitious for the time remaining.

With approximately two-thirds of the slipways hidden under the concrete and tarmac of a 1980s car park, it was uncertain how much of their early twentieth-century composition might still survive. The pressing spring 2012 deadline left no time for extensive exploratory excavations, so HPPA adopted a strategy of minimal intervention, proposing the removal of only the uppermost layers of recent material, then protecting the remaining fabric of the slipways with a new hard landscape. This approach avoided compromising the archaeology, leaving options open for future redevelopment and restoration.

Though their design for a floating halo of light was not be realised, HPPA continued to explore the theme of illumination, seeking alternative means to communicate the imposing scale of the *Olympic*-class liners. Echoing the original concept design, the outlines of the ships were once again laid directly onto the slipways' surface, as though the two ships had left their footprints fossilised in the island's slobland. HPPA looked at a variety of materials for realising this ghostly perimeter, including a line of LedStones that could be laid between the granite pavers. Made largely from recycled glass and filled with LEDs, these translucent crystalline blocks bore the appearance of glowing blocks of ice, adding another element to the narrative.

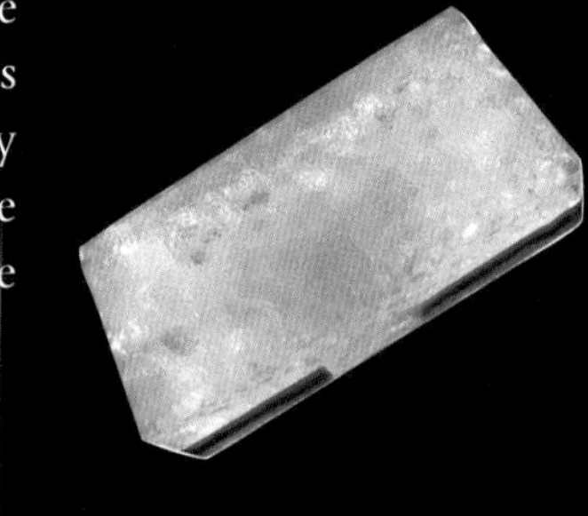

OPPOSITE:
Like ranks of ceremonial pylons lining the approach to some ancient temple, the location of the final light masts corresponded to the Arrol Gantry's originals. The regular spacing lends some sense of perspective to the long vistas up and down the slipways' smooth surfaces, with their minimal raised interventions. Illumination draws the eye to the three key features: the masts, the bow blocks and the ships' outlines.

A ghostly apparition of the Arrol Gantry, the spotlight concept renders offered a fine spectacle, but the graphic density of the beams would have been largely dependent on prevailing light and weather conditions. This idea was also inherently limited by only being able to lend its narrative weight to the site at night, and so other options were duly sought.

Seeking to convey the scale of both the ships and the structure in which they were made, HPPA also investigated means for evoking memories of the Arrol Gantry. Measuring 840 feet (256 metres) long, 240 feet (73 metres) wide, and 228 feet (64 metres) tall to the top of its uppermost crane, the giant gantry had been constructed specifically to accommodate *Titanic* and her sisters and thus formed an integral part of their story. The team first proposed placing powerful recessed spotlights along the slipways, corresponding to the positions of the original gantry stanchions. At night these would send beams of light up to 30 metres into the sky, with the density of the beams increasing in humid conditions. Though undeniably dramatic, various technical and safety issues associated with placing such powerful lights at ground level made this unworkable within the context of historic slips.

The requirement to raise the level of the plaza above the slipways for flood prevention created a stepped profile that the new glowing LED outlines were flexible enough to navigate. Visitors could now survey the slipways from the plaza's edge, before descending stairs or ramps to take their first steps on the original surface of the shipyard.

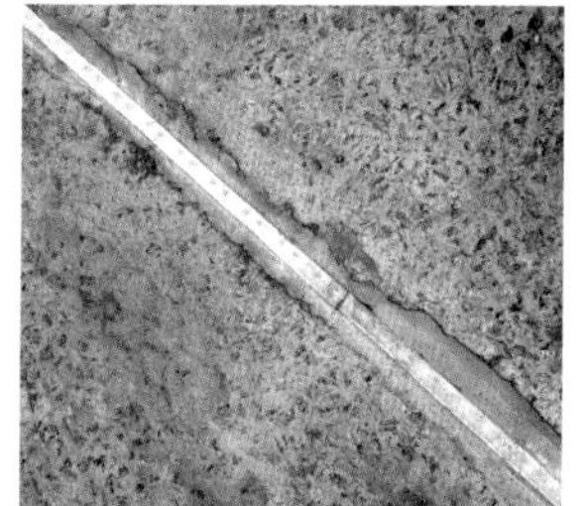

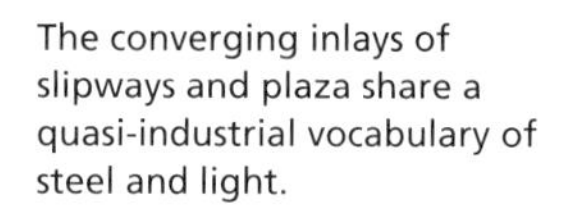

The converging inlays of slipways and plaza share a quasi-industrial vocabulary of steel and light.

Preserved in plan

The final slipway scheme saw the recurring concepts resolved as a series of careful interventions that preserved the character and authenticity of the former shipyard. The full-sized outlines of *Titanic* and *Olympic* were inlaid as fine lines of steel-mounted LED strips, whose aesthetic was more in sympathy with the surviving bogie rails embedded in the concrete. The permanent procession of slender steel light-masts could maintain the lofty aura of the Arrol Gantry all day and in all weathers, replacing the variable beams of the spotlight concept with bold columns of constant LEDs. The result is a post-industrial landscape that offers a canvas for public gatherings on a scale as grand as the great liners it evokes.

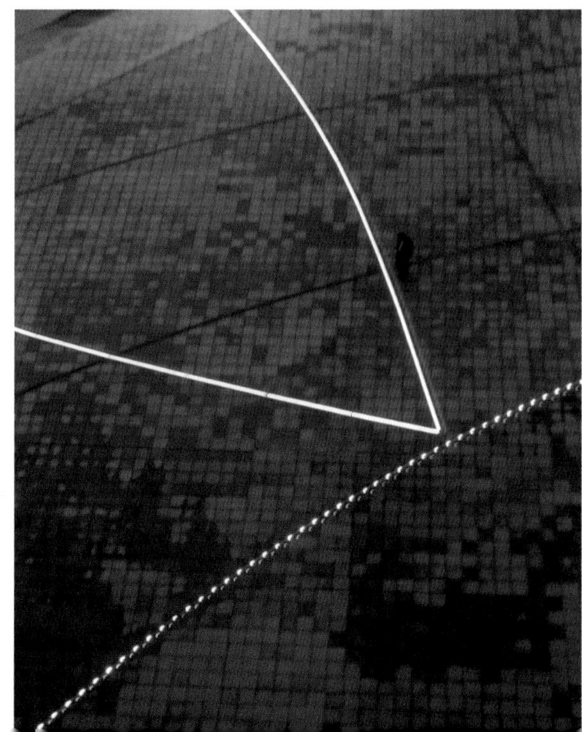

Leaving the original working finish of the upper slipways intact, the later accretions of concrete covering the lower reaches were stripped away and replaced with site-specific installations. The former No. 3 slip, from which *Titanic*'s hull once rose, was relaid in granite pavers, across which the full-size composite plans of the liner's external decks can now be traced in lines of lighter stone. Simple steel and timber benches occupy the same positions as the ship's original deck seating, where passengers would once have sat to watch the Atlantic foaming in *Titanic*'s wake. All around, the rusted forest of steel light masts provides a partial incarnation of the Arrol Gantry, within which these plans were realised.

The most prominent features on the slipways, the sheer drop down the sides of the two concrete bow blocks or 'tongues' presented a potential hazard for visitors. HPPA's elegant design solution was to frame the original fabric with a tall balustrade of laminated glass, which could then double as a moving memorial tablet. Intended to encourage people to reflect upon the human aspect of the tragedy, the glass panels also offer more literal reflections of their surroundings.

Acts of remembrance

While the pale outlines of No. 3 slip present the scale of *Titanic*'s engineering, the sensitive treatment of No. 2 slip conveys the extent of the human tragedy. Of the 2,224 passengers and crew recorded by the British Board of Trade, some 1,514 perished in the North Atlantic, making this one of the greatest maritime disasters of all time. However, *Titanic*'s casualties were not spread evenly amongst the classes, with survival rates varying dramatically according to gender, age and status. HPPA created a stark diagram of the disaster by dividing No. 3 slip into four pairs of turf-and-timber strips, whose varying widths correspond to the survival rates within the ship's social demographic. This separation of survivors and the dead is repeated on the tall glass balustrades framing the two concrete bow blocks. Between them they faithfully record the names of all the passengers and crew, along with those of the workmen who died during *Titanic*'s construction. These two poignant acts of remembrance complete the schemes' narrative arc, bringing *Titanic*'s life story full circle, from its slipway to the memory of its sinking.

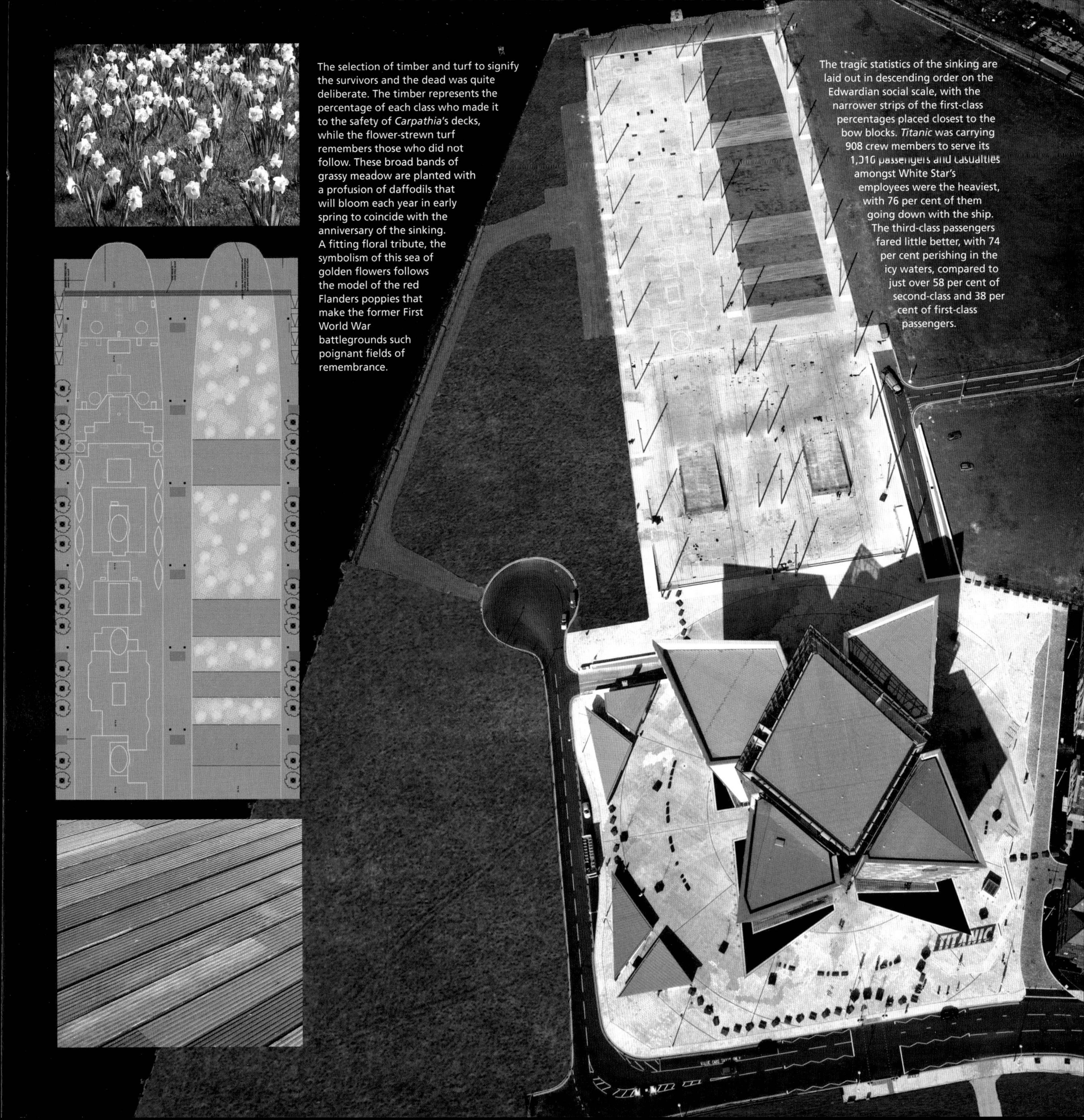

The selection of timber and turf to signify the survivors and the dead was quite deliberate. The timber represents the percentage of each class who made it to the safety of *Carpathia*'s decks, while the flower-strewn turf remembers those who did not follow. These broad bands of grassy meadow are planted with a profusion of daffodils that will bloom each year in early spring to coincide with the anniversary of the sinking. A fitting floral tribute, the symbolism of this sea of golden flowers follows the model of the red Flanders poppies that make the former First World War battlegrounds such poignant fields of remembrance.

The tragic statistics of the sinking are laid out in descending order on the Edwardian social scale, with the narrower strips of the first-class percentages placed closest to the bow blocks. *Titanic* was carrying 908 crew members to serve its 1,316 passengers and casualties amongst White Star's employees were the heaviest, with 76 per cent of them going down with the ship. The third-class passengers fared little better, with 74 per cent perishing in the icy waters, compared to just over 58 per cent of second-class and 38 per cent of first-class passengers.

TITANIC CITY
LARGEST
MAY
CLANGING

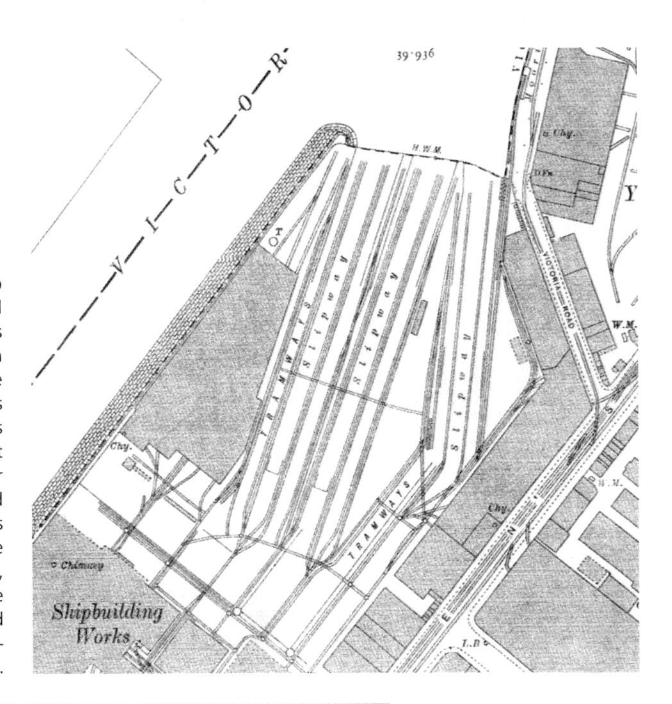

This Ordnance Survey map of 1921 shows the original extent of the metal rails that remain embedded in the concrete of the slipways. These tram lines were the North Yard's umbilical cord, connecting it to Harland & Wolff's wider operations, which extended across much of Queen's Island. They allowed large pre-fabricated elements, such as funnels and turbine casings, to be transported from workshop to fitting-out wharf with ease.

A comparison between photographs of the same rails taken in 2009 (right) and 2012 (left) illustrates how HPPA's restrained design helped preserve the raw industrial character of the surviving slipways. All soil and vegetation were removed and any subsidence remedied by lifting, then relaying the concrete fragments at their original level. Any gaps were filled with resin-bound gravel to reduce possible trip hazards, leaving the lines of rails to stand out against the coarse scrubbed concrete.

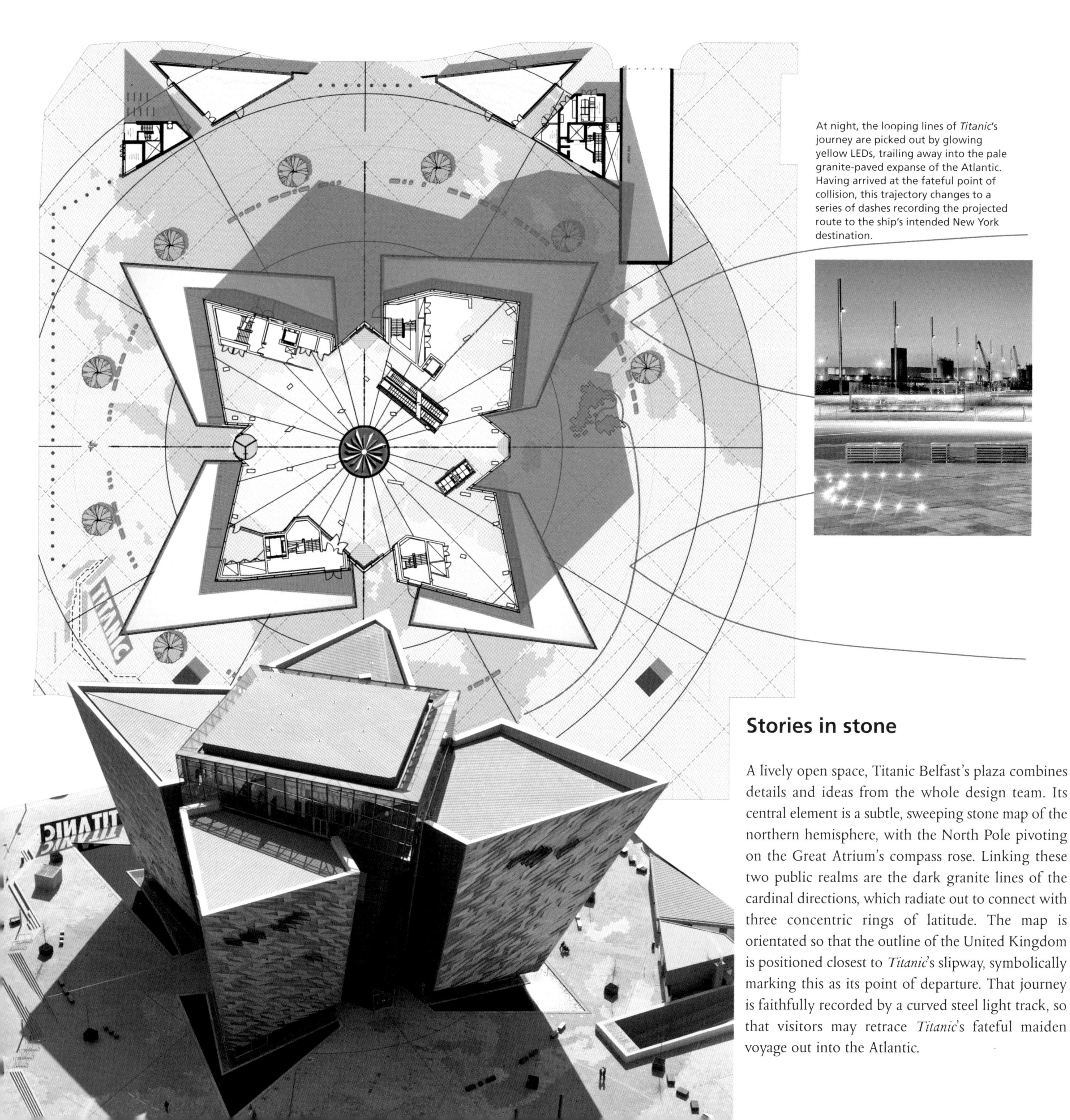

At night, the looping lines of *Titanic*'s journey are picked out by glowing yellow LEDs, trailing away into the pale granite-paved expanse of the Atlantic. Having arrived at the fateful point of collision, this trajectory changes to a series of dashes recording the projected route to the ship's intended New York destination.

Stories in stone

A lively open space, Titanic Belfast's plaza combines details and ideas from the whole design team. Its central element is a subtle, sweeping stone map of the northern hemisphere, with the North Pole pivoting on the Great Atrium's compass rose. Linking these two public realms are the dark granite lines of the cardinal directions, which radiate out to connect with three concentric rings of latitude. The map is orientated so that the outline of the United Kingdom is positioned closest to *Titanic*'s slipway, symbolically marking this as its point of departure. That journey is faithfully recorded by a curved steel light track, so that visitors may retrace *Titanic*'s fateful maiden voyage out into the Atlantic.

'CQD CQD SOS SOS CQD DE MGY': John G. Phillips's Morse-code message combined the old maritime distress signal, CQD, with the newly introduced SOS, together with *Titanic*'s own call sign, MGY.

Combining the themes of cartography and communication, the plaza's map is overlaid with a halo of dot- and dash-shaped benches arranged in prescribed groups. Designed by CivicArts, this ring of outdoor seating records the final Morse-code wireless message sent from the stricken *Titanic* by the Marconi wireless operator, John G. Phillips. Guarding the plaza's perimeter, the compulsory security barriers were discretely integrated into the narrative by HPPA, who detailed them as sculpted blocks of glass-reinforced concrete that double as public seating. Their irregular hardwood bench-tops are randomly rotated along the line, like the abstract drifting fragments of an ice floe.

Having begun as an irregular crystalline form set amidst a simple water garden, Titanic Belfast had evolved into a muscular set of hulls hovering above its dark fringe of reflection pools. These pools bring water to the building's foot, strengthening the allusions to naval architecture and presenting a smooth mirror that magnifies its facades in the still hours of the early morning.

With their waters just 50 millimetres deep, the reflection pools do not pose a significant hazard. Nonetheless, distracted visitors staring skywards at the glittering facades are spared wet feet by the discreetly textured borders that alert them to their proximity to the edges. Detailed by Todd Architects, this band of coarsely chiselled granite echoes the rippling impressionistic patterns of the reflected cladding as a breeze disturbs the water's surface.

Writing on the walls

The wide, paved expanse of the plaza was kept as clean and uncluttered as possible in order to preserve uninterrupted views of Titanic Belfast and the historic drawing offices it faces. CivicArts took the two substantial concrete flues that ventilate the car parks below and clad them with a series of eight laminated glass panels, illustrating the evolution of Queen's Island through a timeline of delicately tinted historic maps. Together with the 700 square metres of bold window graphics created by Tandem Design, this is a mine of local information that remains freely accessible to every casual visitor, forming an outdoor gallery of cartography and social history that further enriches the public realm.

Though it stands as tall as a ten-storey building, the visual mass of Titanic Belfast is greatly reduced by the degree of separation provided by the glass skirt ringing its ground floor. Tandem's gallery of trades and silhouetted shipyard workers turns this glass ring into an informative frieze of facts and figures. Illuminated at night, the facades' combination of frosted glass and anodised aluminium transforms the building into a beacon for Belfast.

Bold signature

Cut from 30-millimetre-thick steel plates, similar to those used to fabricate the great ship herself, the striking graphic identity of the plaza's entry sign announces 'TITANIC' to the world. Set within a steel canvas 4.5 metres tall and 15 metres long, the fretted letters are large enough to allow visitors to step into character, as it were, for a memorable photo opportunity, while helping frame iconic views of the building behind. Designed by Eric Kuhne, the sign's sans-serif typeface references those typefaces originally employed when applying lettering to *Titanic*'s side and stern. The sign's subtractive approach to letter-making also acts as a subtle tribute to the missing, while its graphic shadow, gradually italicised by the sun tracking across the sky, marks the passage of time. Capturing the scale, solidity and strength of the immense sheets of steel once stacked here around the island's platers' sheds, this bold sign represents a steely tribute to the thousands of workers who laboured long upon *Titanic*'s slip.

Constructed by BSK Engineering in County Tyrone, the sign made its 50-mile journey to the site in one piece. Having crisply fretted the letters from eight steel panels using an industrial laser beam, the fabricators then allowed the sign's steel to rust naturally before sealing it with a clear lacquer. Anchored by a series of hidden welded supports, the base of the sign is screened in a shallow trough of gravel that absorbs the run-off from the rusted surface.

A fitting figurehead

The final piece of public art to grace the plaza was to be the elegant bronze *Titanica.* Sculpted by the Irish artist Rowan Gillespie, her human scale and sweeping pose were inspired both by his friend's collection of salvaged ship's figureheads, and by his own boyhood memories of the leaping mascot on his father's Jaguar. A sculptor of international renown, Gillespie is a rarity in the modern art world, for he produces his works in their entirety, from lost-wax modelling through to casting and finishing, within his own foundry. Mounted on her crisp patinated plinth of bolted metal, *Titanica*'s organic, flowing lines form a contrast with the hard-edged aesthetic of the hulls and their jagged aluminium cladding. There is a duality to her character, with her profile emphasising her graceful swept-back arms as though she lies frozen in mid-dive. But when viewed from directly ahead, she instead presents darker echoes of crucifixion and hoped-for resurrection. Combining grace and grief, Gillespie's slender statue offers a fitting monument to the triumph and tragedy of *Titanic.*

A grand opening

H&W

The launch

The stepped plaza edge formed a natural podium for the succession of politicians and city worthies who spoke to the assembled crowd of cameras, beaming their message around the world. Behind them, the rusted patina of the *Titanic* sign provided a constant reminder of the ship whose enduring fame had now found a focal point in the very yard where it was made.

Finished on time and on budget, Titanic Belfast opened its doors on 31st March 2012, exactly a hundred years after the famous liner was completed. The world's largest *Titanic*-themed visitor attraction, the project had taken over seven years to progress from concept through construction to completion, absorbing over £97 million in the process. The line of high-profile dignitaries arrayed to address the world's media underlined the pride felt by both city and province for their newest landmark. This was concrete proof that Belfast could rebuild its shattered tourism industry and reclaim its industrial heritage as an asset to its future economy. The words of the First Minister, Peter Robinson, summed up the groundswell of optimism that day: 'Titanic Belfast marks not just a commemoration of the internationally recognised story but a new beginning for Northern Ireland on the world stage.'

The deliberate symbolism of the ribbon-cutting ceremony reinforced the aspirations for Titanic Belfast to be a neutral, non-sectarian landmark, pointing a course towards a bright future, away from the city's troubled past. Representing unionist and nationalist sides of the Northern Irish political world, First Minister Peter Robinson and Deputy First Minister Martin McGuinness simultaneously cut the broad blue ribbon swathing the monumental sign, marking the building's official opening. Titanic Belfast's Chief Executive, Tim Husbands, led the enthusiastic applause that greeted this historic moment.

The body language of Enterprise Minister Arlene Foster reflected the overriding tone of the event, which encouraged the people of Belfast to embrace the new attraction as a means of drawing the community together. The First and Deputy First Ministers' joint cutting of the ribbon was echoed again inside, when they riveted the commemorative plaque to one of the atrium's lofty steel columns.

Artefacts of the future, Titanic Belfast's first-day tickets carried echoes of the now-rare and highly prized original invitations to *Titanic's* own launch, adding to the sense that people were taking part in a memorable moment in history.

Launch
OF
White Star Royal Mail Triple-Screw Steamer
"TITANIC"
At BELFAST,
Wednesday, 31st May, 1911, at 12-15 p.m.
Admit Bearer.

The fact that nearly 100,000 advance tickets were sold in the three months leading up to the grand opening gives some indication of the international enthusiasm and anticipation surrounding Titanic Belfast. The sheer authenticity of the site, and the way in which the architecture responded to it, marked this as something very special amongst the other exhibits and memorials being opened in ports with *Titanic* connections, such as Liverpool and Cherbourg. As Deputy First Minister Martin McGuinness reflected, '*Titanic* is such a global story that it is only right and fitting that it is properly remembered in the city of its birth.'

Having opened Titanic Belfast with all due ceremony, the various dignitaries were treated to a guided tour of the building, including the impressive new banqueting hall that was destined to become one of the city's most sought-after events venues. Here Deputy First Minister Martin McGuinness signals his approval of the fine Northern Irish craftsmanship invested in the sweeping Grand Staircase.

The attraction was booked solid for the first two weeks, including the deeply symbolic weekend of 14th–15th April, which would see the centennial commemorations of the fateful sinking. The cultural events programme sensitively celebrated the rediscovered civic pride in Belfast's engineering prowess, while creating an appropriately moving commemoration for the many hundreds who lost their lives when the mighty ship went down.

The exhibition designers had consciously appealed to the widest possible audience, ranging from schoolchildren to pensioners, and the faces of the young people leaving the galleries suggested they had struck the correct balance between information and entertainment. The oldest visitor on the first day was 105-year-old Belfast man Cyril Quigley, who had actually witnessed *Titanic* leaving Belfast Lough ahead of her maiden voyage a hundred years previously.

H & W

The complex architecture of Titanic Belfast presented an interesting challenge for the show's designers, Seeper, who were more accustomed to beaming their displays onto flat, blank surfaces. The angular geometry of all 3,000 three-dimensional panels had to be mapped using a laser scanner before the bespoke projections could be devised. The designers exploited the patterns of the panels, using them as virtual building blocks for constructing ships, engines and seascapes that dissolved into one another.

Projections and pyrotechnics

A week after its official opening, Titanic Belfast was again under the spotlight, as its aluminium hulls became the canvas for a spectacular light show, complete with music and fireworks. Commissioned by Belfast City Council and the Northern Ireland Tourist Board, the event on 7th April was attended by a crowd of around 30,000 people, who watched a succession of animation sequences beamed across the aluminium cladding using a technique called 'architectural projection mapping'. Amidst streams of spluttered orange flares, like the sparks from a welder's torch, the panels appeared to peel back to reveal the pounding cogs and gears of some immense maritime machinery. Titanic Belfast had truly come to life.

‘*Titanic* belongs to Belfast.’ Dr Robert Ballard

Ballard in Belfast

The story of *Titanic*’s sinking had already achieved legendary status in the years after the disaster, but the rediscovery of her wreck in 1985 led to a massive resurgence of interest in the ship that had come to symbolise her age. Her discoverer, Dr Robert Ballard, had visited Titanic Belfast during its construction and been greatly impressed by the care being invested in telling the story of both the ship and the city that built her. As a man who had dedicated 12 years of his life to finding *Titanic*, it was only fitting that Ballard should return to Belfast for the centenary of the sinking on 14th–15th April, and deliver the Memorial Lecture to commemorate those fateful events. Staged against the dramatic backdrop of the Grand Staircase in the packed banqueting hall, this moving presentation was followed the next day by a talk for children and families entitled ‘Into the Deep’, aimed at inspiring the next generation of great oceanographers.

The memorial weekend witnessed the historic reunion of Dr Robert Ballard and the diving engineer, Jean-Louis Michel, who had led the respective American and French contingents of the successful 1985 search for *Titanic*. Having spent ten days conducting a sonar sweep of the seabed, Michel was obliged to return the research ship, *Le Suroît*, to port for other duties. A handful of French scientists were able to transfer to Ballard’s ship, the *Knorr*, which would ultimately locate *Titanic*’s debris field.

Queen's Island

One hundred and sixty-three years after this reclaimed land was renamed to honour a visiting monarch, Queen's Island played proud host to her reigning descendant. Her Majesty the Queen visited Belfast on 27th June 2012 as part of her nationwide diamond-jubilee tour. This was only her second two-day visit to Northern Ireland since her silver jubilee tour in 1977, which had been conducted in a heightened climate of sectarian tension and with the real threat of terrorism. Now warmly received by the assembled crowds, this historic royal visit was filled with potent symbols of the reconciliation brought about by the ongoing peace process, with Her Majesty shaking hands with Deputy First Minister Martin McGuinness. The royal party's itinerary included a visit to Titanic Belfast on Queen's Island, which saw its greatest gathering of civic leaders and dignitaries since the grand opening in March. Her Majesty and the Duke of Edinburgh were given a guided tour of the galleries by Titanic Belfast's Chief Executive, Tim Husbands, including a trip on the aerial ride that recreated a shipyard that had built so many vessels bearing the 'HMS' prefix.

As well as unveiling a plaque to commemorate her historic visit, Her Majesty was introduced to many of the key people who had helped make Titanic Belfast a reality. These included (from right to left) concept architect Eric Kuhne of CivicArts, Paul Crowe of Todd Architects and Conal Harvey, Director of Harcourt Developments & Deputy Chairman of Titanic Quarter. Together with Pat Doherty, Harvey had been a major driving force behind the project since its inception.

Staged on 8th September, the BBC *Proms in the Park* entertained an audience of 7,000 with its blend of classical and contemporary music performed by a stellar line-up including acclaimed tenor Noah Stewart (pictured left, courtesy of BBC Northern Ireland). The sheer scale of the slipways was rapidly making them the public venue of choice for Belfast's cultural calendar. The new banqueting hall, whose glass-walled viewing platforms offer panoramic views of the illuminated ships' outlines at night, was also in great demand. From cultural events to corporate hospitality, Titanic Belfast was becoming the living landmark that its designers had always aspired to create.

Cultural Quarter

Expectations that Titanic Belfast would become the lynchpin of Titanic Quarter proved well founded, for the attraction and its adjoining slipways played host to a succession of successful public events in its maiden year. It hosted a special stage of the 2012 Donnelly Group Circuit of Ireland Rally on Good Friday, followed by the impressive light show on 7th April, and the musical extravaganza of *MTV Titanic Sounds* a week later. The summer saw the slipways filled for *Land of Giants*, billed as the 'biggest outdoor arts celebration ever staged in Northern Ireland', with some 500 acrobats and dancers. The BBC's *Proms in the Park* completed this programme, adding classical music to this mix of cultural riches.

Brighton hip-hop duo Rizzle Kicks were amongst the acts taking to the stage for *MTV Titanic Sounds*, whose lighting gantries framed the dramatic silhouette of Titanic Belfast behind. The free event on 13th April 2012 attracted a crowd of 16,000, who were entertained by an international array of artists including Olly Murs, Pixie Lott and Sean Paul.

'It is really quite phenomenal.' James Cameron, Director

Cameron had used his own replica of the Grand Staircase as the backdrop for several memorable scenes in *Titanic*, and his commanding stance on the banqueting hall's incarnation of the iconic stair suggests he was quite at home within the setting for the launch.

Making the director's cut

Titanic has been the subject of innumerable stories, films, songs and poems since its sinking in 1912, but the dramatic impact of James Cameron's 1997 epic film exceeded all that had gone before it. Winner of 11 Academy Awards, *Titanic* remains one of the highest-grossing box-office successes of all time, and still had the power to pull in the crowds when rereleased in 3D to coincide with the centenary of the maiden voyage. Together with his producer, Jon Landau, Cameron made a three-day visit to Titanic Belfast in September 2012 to promote the release of the film on 3D Blu-ray disc. After all, where better to launch the new cut to the world than in the birthplace of the great ship? The film's promotion in the building continued after Cameron's departure with his six-month loan of original props from the film for display, including the impressive ship's wheel, which he had kept as a personal souvenir.

A place for peacemakers

In the wake of high-profile visits by renowned filmmakers and oceanographers, Titanic Belfast's reputation as an international stage continued to soar as it witnessed the honouring of a very special guest. The Ireland Funds chose the banqueting hall as the venue in which to present Hillary Clinton with a lifetime achievement award, saluting her commitment to peace and reconciliation in Northern Ireland over her two decades as First Lady, a US senator and Secretary of State. Titanic Belfast was now emphatically on the world map as a place where history could be made, not just recorded.

The 500 luncheon guests were drawn from all sides of the Northern Irish community and included business, civic, community and cultural leaders. The roll call included the First Minister and Deputy First Minister of Northern Ireland, along with members of the diplomatic world, the sporting world and the entertainment industry.

The occasion included a rare reunion between politicians David Trimble (left) and John Hume (centre), whose successful efforts in helping bring about the Good Friday Agreement resulted in their being jointly awarded the Nobel Peace Prize in 1998.

Belfast: de Titanic komt weer thuis

Noord-Ierse hoofdstad is trots op geboorteplaats schip

Door een project dat katholieken en protestanten scheidde, nu een product van gezamenlijke trots. De Titanic maakt Belfast weer groot. Vandaag opent een interactief museum de deuren voor het publiek.

GLOBAL TRAVELER

small nations big festivals

From Cat Throwing To Titanic Tragedy, Europe's Smaller Nations Offer Up World Class Celebrations

fast à l'heure Titanic

A sense of proportions

The epic tale of the Titanic is putting the pride back into Belfast, discovers Susan Swarbrick

'It's the greatest story never told. The world had Titanic for 10 days. We had her for three years'

Världen

Katastrofskeppet pr

Let the new Titanic be your gateway to Ireland

Belfast, un museo per il TITANIC

travel

Titanic legend lives on

Titanic

La puissance d'une légende

Il y a un siècle, dans la nuit du 14 au 15 avril 1912, le *Titanic* heurtait un iceberg et som-

REISE

BIRMA Ein verschlossenes Land öffnet sich – Seite R2

SCHOTTLAND

Als alle Spiegel zerbrachen

Cover story

Voyage of hope

A century after *Titanic* set sail from Belfast prior to her tragic maiden journey, a £97m tribute to the ship and her makers is almost ready. **Simon Calder** reports

Titanic Town

EXPRESS STYLES

styles

modes de vie

MUSÉE AMARRÉ

Convention international

Circulation: 15.085

Titanic Belfast: Die vielleicht spannendste neue Location des Jahres

REISEN&ENTDECKEN

Vom Ende eines Traumes

Proud to launch the Titanic tale

Ein sensationeller neuer Museumsbau, der schon vor seiner Eröffnung Kultstatus besitzt, bietet nun einen Anlass, sowohl das legendenumwobene Schiff als auch die Stadt, in der die Titanic vor 100 Jahren gebaut wurde, näher kennenzulernen

Titanic Belfast Building

Ein neues Wahrzeichen für die Stadt

QUATRE PROUES AUX QUATRE VENTS

Belfast ademt TITANIC

Responsibility for delivering the *Titanic* experience fell to Titanic Belfast's CEO, Tim Husbands, and his deputy, Judith Owens. Hand-picked from thousands of applicants, the enthusiasm of their new staff ensured that guests from around the world received the warmest welcome. Effectively placed in the role of ambassadors for Northern Ireland, the team's efforts were recognised when Tim Husbands was named Belfast's Businessperson of the Year, 2012, while Titanic Belfast received the accolade for Best Hospitality, 2012.

A global success story

Before its official opening on 31st March 2012, Titanic Belfast was set an annual target of 425,000 visitors a year. Within six months it had played host to over 500,000. The universal appeal of the *Titanic* brand, coupled with the significance of the 2012 centenary, had made this the standout Signature Project in Northern Ireland's campaign to resurrect its tourist industry. The story was local, but the appeal was global. Titanic Belfast attracted some 20,000 guests from the USA, 6,000 from Canada, 2,000 from China and even 20 from Palestine. They came to be immersed in an experience that delivered what its designers and champions set out to achieve: to bring the linked histories of city and ship to life with the greatest authenticity. Their years of designing, planning and building have left a legacy that everyone can share. The city that gave *Titanic* to the world can now welcome the world to Titanic Belfast.

The half-millionth visitor to Titanic Belfast arrived from overseas, but had strong local ties. Born in east Belfast, retired teacher Lynda Price was the great-granddaughter of a Harland & Wolff shipyard worker. She had left Northern Ireland in 1976 and settled in Canada.

The *Titanic* name was already a familiar component of Belfast's recovering tourist industry, but Titanic Belfast gave it a central focal point from which the wider city could be explored. The linkage of historic docks, pump houses and other places of interest has created a critical mass of *Titanic* activities that no other city can match.

CITY

‘Titanic’s story is infused with romance, pathos and glory, and there’s no better place to tell it than Belfast.’ Dr Robert Ballard

TITANIC BELFAST

COLLEAGUES & CONTRIBUTORS

CLIENTS

Overall Client:
Titanic Foundation Ltd
www.titanic-foundation.org

Design and Build Contractor:
Harcourt Construction (NI) Ltd
www.harcourtdevelopments.com

Operator:
Titanic Belfast Ltd
www.titanicbelfast.com

FUNDERS & DONORS

Department of Enterprise, Trade and Investment
www.detini.gov.uk

Northern Ireland Tourist Board
www.nitb.com

Belfast City Council
www.belfastcity.gov.uk

Belfast Harbour Commissioners
www.belfast-harbour.co.uk

Titanic Quarter Ltd
www.titanic-quarter.com

THE DESIGN TEAM

Concept Design Architects:
CivicArts/Eric R. Kuhne & Associates
www.civicarts.com

Lead Consultants/Architects:
Todd Architects
www.toddarch.com

Exhibition Designers:
Event Communications Ltd
www.eventcomm.com

Concept Interior Designers:
CivicArts/Eric R. Kuhne & Associates
www.civicarts.com

Interior Designers:
Kay Elliott
www.kayelliott.co.uk

Concept Landscape Designers:
CivicArts/Eric R. Kuhne & Associates
www.civicarts.com

Landscape Architects:
Heber-Percy & Parker Architects
www.hpandp.co.uk

Exhibition Designers:
Event Communications
www.eventcomm.com

Planning Consultants:
Turley Associates
www.turleyassociates.co.uk

Tourism Consultants:
CHL Consulting Group
www.chl.ie

Graphic Designers:
Tandem Design
www.tandemdesign.co.uk

ENGINEERING, CONSTRUCTION & SERVICES CONSULTANTS

Structural, Civil and Fire Engineers:
RPS Group plc
www.rpsgroup.com

Building Services Engineers:
AECOM
www.aecom.com

Project and Cost Management:
Cyril Sweett/Sweett Group
www.sweettgroup.com

Facade Contractors:
Metallbau Früh
www.metallbau-frueh.de

Facade Manufacturers:
EDM Spanwall Facades Ltd
www.edmproducts.com

Lighting Designers/Lighting Strategists:
Sutton Vane Associates
www.sva.co.uk

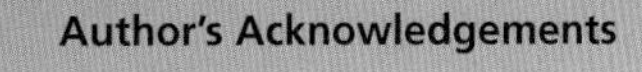

Author's Acknowledgements

I would like to thank the following people for their generous assistance in compiling this intricate story of Titanic Belfast. The time they kindly spared to answer my many questions and image requests has made this book immeasurably richer. I hope the result does their labours justice:

Rodney McCullough, Titanic Quarter
Michael Counahan, CHL Consulting
Eric R. Kuhne, CivicArts
Mark Evans, CivicArts
Paul Crowe, Todd Architects
Angus Waddington, Todd Architects
Paul McGettigan, RPS Group
David Ross, RPS Group
Adrian Grimshaw, Sweett Group
Steve Lumby, Event Communications
Victoria Kingston, Event Communications
David Craddock, Kay Elliott
Bernard Parker, Heber-Percy & Parker
James Munro, Heber-Percy & Parker
Paul Louden-Brown FRSA, White Star Line Archive
Conal Harvey, Director of Harcourt Developments & Deputy Chairman of Titanic Quarter

Thanks must also be extended to the three principal photographers, Donal McCann, Christopher Heaney and Christopher Hill, for the reader experiences Titanic Belfast through their skilfully trained lenses.

And last, but by no means least, I must thank this book's designer, Wendy Dunbar, for her constant encouragement during the many patient hours we've spent composing every page. Like the building it records, this book has been a genuine collaboration.

PAUL CATTERMOLE

Principal Exhibition Fit-Out Contractors:
Paragon Creative
www.paragon-creative.co.uk

Acoustic Consultants:
AWN Consulting
www.awnconsulting.com

BREEAM Consultants:
SDS Energy Ltd
www.sdsenergy.com

Wind Consultants:
RWDI Anemos
www.rwdi.com

Construction (Design and Management) Coordinators:
Hasco Europe Ltd
www.hasco-europe.com

Commissioning Managers:
Williams & Shaw
www.williamsandshaw.co.uk

EARLY SIGNATURE PROJECT CONSULTANTS

Lighting Design Consultants:
Bliss Fasman Inc.
www.blissfasman.com

Mechanical and Electrical Consultants:
Tavakoli Associates Ltd
www.talimited.com

Structural Engineers:
RFR Group
www.rfr.fr

Exhibition Costing/Quantity Surveyors:
PT Projects Ltd
www.ptprojects.co.uk

Financial Modelling:
KPMG International
www.kpmg.com

Feasibility, Risk Register and Business Planning:
Colin Stutt Consulting
www.colinstutt.com

Catering Consultants:
Coverpoint Foodservice Consultants
www.coverpoint.co.uk

CLIENT ADVISORS

EC Harris Built Asset Consultancy
www.echarris.com

HLM Architects
www.hlmarchitects.com

Mott MacDonald Group Ltd
www.mottmac.com

Investment Strategy Northern Ireland
www.isni.gov.uk

Picture Credit List

Alphabetically by contributor

Key to abbreviations:

TL – Top Left
TM- Top Middle
TR – Top Right

CL - Centre Left
CM – Centre Middle
CR – Centre Right

BL – Bottom Left
BM – Bottom Middle
BR – Bottom Right

BK – Background
M – Main image
All – All images on page

Author's dedication
For Pamela, Katherine & Eleanor
We'll go there together, one day.

123RF – Royalty Fee Images: 36-BK
Mikey Ashworth/Flickr: 37-CR
Belfast Harbour Commissioners: 13-All, 14-BK, 16-BK, 17-TR, 38-TL
Sylvia Brendel: 152-All
Bernie Brown/bbphotographic.co.uk: 148-BL
The Thomas Carnduff Estate: 110-CM, (Published with kind permission of Sarah Ferris, Literary Executor)
Paul Cattermole/CivicArts: 24-M, 45-BK, 83-TL, 83-TM, 83-TR, 89-BR, 114-BL, 128-TR, 128-BR, 133-BR, 135-BL, 136-BR, 149-BL
CivicArts/Eric R Kuhne & Associates: 1-CM, 3&4, 27-Left All, 27-BM, 28-BK, 29-M, 31-BR, 32-All, 33-TL, 33-TR, 34-All, 33-TR, 33-CM, 33-BR, 36-TL, 36-TR, 36-BR, 36-CL, 37-Tl, 37-TR, 37-BL, 37-BM, 37-BR, 38-CL, 38-CR, 39-All, 40-Top, 40-M, 41-TL, 41-BR, 41-CR, 43-M, 44-All, 46-BK, 48-TL, 48-BL, 48-BM, 49-M, 51-BK, 63-BR, 102-TL, 102-BL, 102-BR, 103-All, 104-TL, 110-TM, 112-All, 113-All, 122-M, 122-TL, 123-All, 124-All, 134-TL
William Cherry/PressEye: 151-TL, 151-M (Courtesy of BBC Northern Ireland)
Michael Counahan/CHL Consulting: 139-BL
Esler Crawford Photography: 10-BK
Didier Descouens/Wikipedia: 35-TL
Rob Durston: 100&101, 110-BR
Engineering, 1911: 122-CR, 125-CR, 129-TM-Lower
Mark Evans/CivicArts: 44-All, 128-TM, 131-BL
Event Communications Ltd: 25-All, 26-TL, 26-BL, 78-All, 79-All, 81-M, 85-TL, 85-BR, 87-TR, 87-BL, 89-TR, 93-Tl, 93-TR
Paul Faith/PA: 153-BR
Adrian Grimshaw/Sweett Group: 55-M, 59-CR-Upper
Harrison Photography: 153-M, 153-CM
Harland and Wolff Heavy Industries Ltd: 16-TR, 16-CR, 17-BK, 19-BM, 22-BR
Heber-Percy & Parker: 125-TL, 125-BL, 126-All, 129-TM-Upper, 131-CL, 135-BR
Christopher Heaney/Titanic Belfast: 6&7, 30&31, 62&63, 63-TR, 66-TR, 67-M, 67-BM, 69-TL, 69-M, 70-TL, 70-TR, 71-M, 71-BM, 72-All, 73-All, 74&75, 84-TL, 86-M, 87-BR, 88-M, 88-TR, 0-BL, 90-BR, 91-M, 91-BL, 93-BR, 94, 95-BM, 96, 97-All, 98&99, 104-BR, 111-BR, 120&121, 121-CR, 127-B, 128-M, 129-M, 130-M, 132&133, 134-CR, 135-M, 137, 138-M, 138-TM, 138-CL, 139-All, 140&141, 142-M, 143-M, 143-BL, 144-TL, 144-M, 145-TL, 145-M, 146&147, 148-M, 154-BK, 160
Christopher Hill Photographic: 52&53, 57-M, 57-TR, 58-CL, 58-TR, 59-TL, 59-TR, 59-BR, 60, 98-BL, 136-M, 147-TM, 147-CM
Christopher Hill Photographic/Todd Architects: 2&3, 81-BL, 89-CL, 89-BL, 90-M, 110-M, 118&119, 127-T, 131-M, 134-BL, 150-TR, 155-BR, 156&157, 158&159
Elaine Hill: 85-BL, 87-TL, 93-BL
Marie-Therese Hurson/Harrison Photography: 149-M, 146-BR
Kay Elliott: 105-All, 107-TR, 109-BL, 114-BR, 115-TL, 115-TM, 115-BK, 116-TL
Darren Kidd/Presseye: 151-All
Linen Hall Library: 15-TL, 15-M
Paul Louden-Brown/White Star Line Archive: 41-TL
Davide Mazzaglia: 136-CR
George McAllister: 107-TL
Donal McCann/Harcourt Construction (NI) Ltd: 66-CL, 68-M, 68-TR, 69-TR
Donal McCann Photography: Cover, 64&65, 76&77, 80, 81-BR, 82-M, 82-BL, 83-M, 89-TL, 91-BR, 92, 94-TL,106-All, 107-M, 108-All, 109-TL, 109-TR, 111-BL, 111-TR, 115-BL, 115-BR, 115-CR, 116-TM, 116-TR, 116-CR, 116-BL, 116-BR, 117-All, 130-BR
Donal McCann/Titanic Quarter Ltd: 4&5, 8, 61-M
Alf McCreary: 14-BL
Alex McGreevy/Titanic Belfast Ltd: 155-M, 155-TR
Noel Molloy/Harcourt Construction (NI) Ltd: 54-TL, 54-BK
Monuments and Building Record (MBR), NI: 21-BK (Taggart)
Murray O'Laoire Architects: 26-CR
National Museums Northern Ireland Collection, Ulster Folk & Transport Museum: 9 (HOYFM.HW .H1560), 11-BK (HOYFM.HW .H1721), 12-BK (BELUM.Y.W.10.46.44), 20-BK (HOYFM.WAG. 3734), 21-TL (Esso Ulidia in Dock), 102-TR (HOYFM.WAG.2079), 144-CR (*Titanic* Launch Ticket)
Nature.com: 42-TM
Northern Ireland Tourist Board (NITB): 154-M
Diana Oxlade: 15-TR
Don Parks/www.iPlayOutside.com: 28-BK
Jonathon Porter/PressEye: 84-BK, 85-TR
Public Domain Images: 131-TL
Public Record Office of Northern Ireland (PRONI): 14-TR, 17-TL, 17-CR, 18&19, 19-TM, 21-TL, 22-M, 133-TR
William H. Rau/Library of Congress: 114-TR
RFR Group: 42-TL, 42-TR, 42-BL, 43-BM
RPS Group: 54-TM, 56-CL, 56-BR, 57-BR, 58-BL, 59-CR-Lower, 70-CR, 70-BR
Angela and Kyle Roesler/karoesler.com: 48-TL-Lower
Bill Smyth Photography: 55-BL
Titanic Quarter Ltd: 23-M, 23-BR, 24-CR, 29-TR, 40-CR
Brian Thompson/PressEye: 143-BR
Todd Architects: 46-TL, 47-All, 48-CL, 48-BR, 49-BM, 50-All, 54-TR, 61-Bl, 61-BR, 63-BK, 66-BL, 66-BM, 66-BR, 111-TL
Turley Associates: 27-TR
wallpaperswide.com: 49-TR
Yzmo/Wikipedia: 33-BM

Published by Titanic Belfast Publications
Originated by Booklink (Dr Claude Costecalde)

Consultant editors,
Dr Claude Costecalde, John Paul Doherty
Historical editor, Paul Louden-Brown
Copy editor, Alicia McAuley
Picture research, Paul Cattermole
Design, Wendy Dunbar
Printed in Slovenia
ISBN 978-0-9576300-0-0